C000005131

The Pictorial History of

Lancashire
County Cricket Club

Keith Hayhurst

First published in Great Britain 2000
by Polar Group Ltd, 9-17 Tuxford Road, Hamilton, Leicester LE4 9TZ

Text copyright © Keith Hayhurst 2000
Design copyright Polar Group Ltd © 2000

The Pictorial History of Lancashire County Cricket Club has been published by
Polar Publishing exclusively for Lancashire CCC.

ISBN 1 899538 16 X

British Library Cataloguing in Publication Data.
A catalogue record for this book is available from the British Library.

Text preparation by Keith Hayhurst
Layout & design by Trevor Hartley
General editing by Julian Baskcomb
Co-ordination by Ken Grime

All rights reserved. No part of this publication may be reproduced or stored in a retrieval
system, or transmitted, in any form or by any means without the prior permission of the
Publishers and Author.

Designed & printed by Polar Group Ltd, 9-17 Tuxford Road, Hamilton, Leicester LE4 9TZ.
Tel: 0116 274 4700

Photographs courtesy of Allsport UK, Neil Cross (Lancashire Evening Post),
Dawson Sports Photography, David Frith, Phil Garlington, Tommy Greenhough, Ken Grime,
Geoff Halliwell, Keith Hayhurst, Phill Heywood, Jeffersons Aerial Photography,
Neil McAlistair, Manchester Evening News, Alan Shepherd, Ron Spriggs, Bill Smith.

*The Publishers and Author have, perhaps inevitably, been unable to trace the sources of
all of the pictures used in this book, but any photographer involved who has been inadvertently
omitted is cordially invited to contact Lancashire CCC in writing providing proof of copyright.*

Foreword

by Clive H. Lloyd CBE

THIS book is the first photographic history of Lancashire County Cricket Club. The author has brought to life all the many characters and great players connected with this famous Club from its early beginning in the middle of the 19th century.

My first appearance for the Club was way back in 1968 under the captaincy of Jack Bond, who inspired us to great feats for Lancashire. My first year at the Club was the final year for those great Lancashire icons Brian Statham, Geoff Pullar and Ken Higgs, but it was the dawning of a new era as younger players emerged. My overseas partner was Farokh Engineer who was one of the finest wicket keepers during that period. We had other quality players like Harry Pilling, Peter Lever, Ken Shuttleworth, Barry Wood, David Lloyd, Jack Simmons, David Hughes, Frank Hayes, Graeme Fowler, Paul Allott and many more who made Lancashire one of the most feared teams in the 70s and 80s. I was also quite honoured to captain the Club for three seasons, at a time when we were going through a transitional phase. My only disappointment during those halcyon days, when we were the best team in the country, was that we never achieved the honour of winning the County Championship. We won every other honour but I live in hope that sooner rather than later we will experience the thrill and pride of winning this elusive trophy.

Several special moments of our successful winning years are captured in this wonderful book and the Lancashire supporters will have many happy moments reminiscing and savouring those great times. The majority of pictures come from Keith Hayhurst's marvellous collection. He is one of the leading collectors of cricket memorabilia and has been main architect in setting up the Club's cricket museum. We are all proud of his untiring efforts. Keith and I have been members of the Lancashire Committee for a number of years, and he was also instrumental in setting up the Former Lancashire Players' Association.

I am positive that those who purchase this historical masterpiece will not only enjoy the unique and exciting images, but also it will become a reference book for many Lancashire cricket supporters.

Clive H Lloyd CBE

Introduction

*"Oh to be in England
Now that April's here"*

OUR summer game has given us so many marvellous cricket characters who are household names in Lancashire homes and it is always interesting to be able to put a face to these names. There are cricketers, forgotten in the mists of time, who played their part in the long history of this famous Club and they deserve their mention in a photographic record.

The earliest-known cricket photographs were taken in the late 1850's; engravings were popular a hundred years before that date, but there is no replacement for an exact likeness by the camera. Included here are rare photographs from the earliest decades in the 1850's and 1860's and in the following pages you will discover a number of scenes never published before.

I have collected cricket photographs for over forty years, particularly those with a Lancashire connection. Today, many have become so rare I believe it is time to share some of these early gems with the many dedicated cricket followers of our great County Cricket Club.

I have concentrated on Lancashire County players, interesting matches at Old Trafford, some cricket memorabilia and the development of the ground.

Many Lancashire cricket followers are interested in the history of the Club, others in the characters of the 'Golden Age' and later years. Debates have frequently developed in the Members' area about the greatest side or the best eleven players. Youth is, perhaps understandably, more interested in modern cricket and the latest success of the team.

The plan was to give each chapter an equal weight but, inevitably, as photography improved, more and better images became available.

I hope the selection delights you, and your favourite players are given due recognition for the great pleasure they have given us all on many a memorable English summer day.

Keith A. Hayhurst

Contents

Dedication
To Anne, my patient wife.
Keith A. Hayhurst

My sincere thanks to Ken Grime for his support and
encouragement, and the arrangement of the
production and printing.
K.A.H.

Lancashire County Cricket Club – Its background and social context

Below: In 1781 a cricket match took place near Manchester. In the City, Richard Arkwright had just opened a five-storey cotton mill. In other parts of Lancashire, rioters were destroying the newly invented spinning machines which threatened their jobs. This year the Sussex painter John Constable was 5 years old, Beethoven 10 years and William Wordsworth 11 years.

IN the *Manchester Journal*, 1st September 1781, there appeared an account of a cricket match played in late August five miles from Manchester. It took place eight years before the first President was installed in the USA and before the French Revolution had started.

Cricket in the north developed more slowly than in the south because of the Industrial Revolution. The crunching wheels of machinery, the shriek of steam boilers, the heavy rumble of carts and regular beat of looms occupied the people of Lancashire. The principal merchants and professional men lived in the city and by the early eighteen hundreds, cricket clubs were being formed including the Manchester club.

At first cricket was mainly the domain of the rich amateurs who paid professional cricketers to join their team. In 1847 the Factory Act restricted work to a 55½ hour week which meant people were free to play and watch sport on a Saturday afternoon.

Cricket grew in popularity as the All England XI toured Manchester. In 1857 the Manchester Cricket Club moved to its fourth site, the present Old Trafford ground and on 12th January 1864 representatives from thirteen Lancashire Clubs met in Manchester to form the Lancashire County Cricket Club.

KAH.

Above: In the early part of the 19th century, cricket in the Manchester area was mainly for the rich until the Factory Act of 1847 gave workers more free time.

Below: Lea Birch was Manchester's leading player, a top class batsman, captain of the Manchester Cricket Club and an accurate under-arm bowler. He became President as well as Hon. Secretary and Treasurer of the Club in 1925. This fine trophy was presented to him by the members in 1831.

Above: **John Lillywhite**, son of the famous England bowler Fred Lillywhite, started his cricket career as a professional playing for Manchester Cricket Club in 1848. Fourteen years later, standing as an umpire, he no-balled Edgar Willsher of the All-England XI six times in succession for unfair round-arm bowling which soon led to a famous change in the laws allowing bowlers to deliver over-arm.

Right: In 1857 the Manchester Cricket Club was asked to move because the site was chosen for the famous Manchester Art Exhibition visited by Queen Victoria, Prince Albert and other royals. Sir Humphrey De Trafford, the owner of the estate, provided another site for the Manchester Cricket Club less than a mile away, the present Old Trafford ground. A plan of the site was drawn up and the annual rent was fixed at £37-6s-6d.

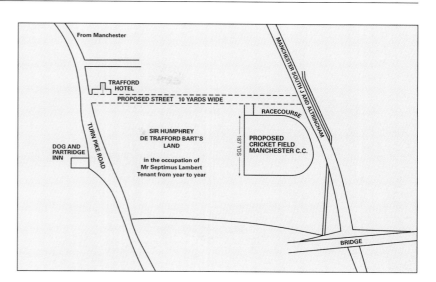

Left: **Thomas Hunt** was run over and killed by a train in 1858. He was leaving the Rochdale ground having played against the United England XI. A Testimonial game was arranged at Old Trafford for his family, the first known benefit for a cricketer in the county.

Right: On leaving the Exhibition site in 1857, a group of Manchester CC members split and formed a club near Eccles named the Western Cricket Club. It existed until the late 1930s. The opening of the ground was reported in the *London Illustrated News* in June 1857.

Above: In 1857 a new pavilion was built on the newly-opened Old Trafford ground. It consisted of a central compartment for dining, 36 feet by 22 feet. It had two wings and a turret surmounting the centre described as a light and elegant structure. The western wing (left) accommodated the amateur players on the ground floor and the upper room for the committee. The professional, Thomas Hunt, resided in the east wing as well as the caterer of the club, Mr Johnson.

Above: Players from the first major match at Old Trafford. In the group photograph standing from the left are **Tom Hayward, Heathfield Stephenson, Julius Caesar, George Parr, James Henry Dark** (proprietor of the Lord's ground and manager of the teams), **George Tarrant, Richard Daft, Robert Tinley** (who took 14 wickets against the England XI) and the tall **John Jackson** who claimed five wickets in each innings for the England XI. **Edgar Willsher** is front *(left)* on the grass.

Right: Spectators in their thousands attended Old Trafford in 1860 to see George Parr's England team, having just returned from a tour of the USA. They were playing another England XI.

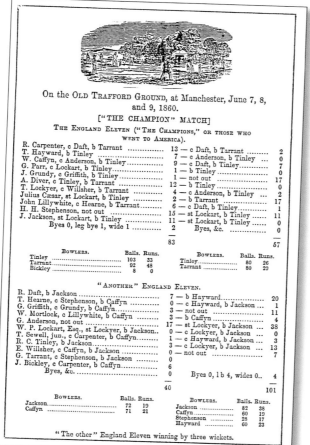

On the OLD TRAFFORD GROUND, at Manchester, June 7, 8, and 9, 1860.

["THE CHAMPION" MATCH]

THE ENGLAND ELEVEN ("THE CHAMPIONS," OR THOSE WHO WENT TO AMERICA).

R. Carpenter, c Daft, b Tarrant 13	— c Daft, b Tarrant	2
T. Hayward, b Tinley 7	— c Anderson, b Tinley ...	0
W. Caffyn, c Anderson, b Tinley............... 9	— c Daft, b Tinley............	7
G. Parr, c Lockart, b Tinley.................... 1	— b Tinley	0
J. Grundy, c Griffith, b Tinley................. 1	— not out	17
A. Diver, c Tinley, b Tarrant 12	— b Tinley	0
T. Lockyer, c Willsher, b Tinley 4	— c Anderson, b Tinley ...	2
Julius Cæsar, st Lockart, b Tinley 2	— b Tarrant	17
John Lillywhite, c Hearne, b Tarrant........ 6	— c Daft, b Tinley............	1
H. H. Stephenson, not out 15	— st Lockart, b Tinley	11
J. Jackson, st Lockart, b Tinley 11	— st Lockart, b Tinley	0
Byes 0, leg bye 1, wide 1 2	Byes, &c.........	0
83		**57**

BOWLERS.	Balls.	Runs.		BOWLERS.	Balls.	Runs.
Tinley	103	33		Tinley	80	26
Tarrant	92	48		Tarrant	80	29
Bickley	8	0				

"ANOTHER" ENGLAND ELEVEN.

R. Daft, b Jackson 7	— b Hayward.................	20
T. Hearne, c Stephenson, b Caffyn 0	— c Hayward, b Jackson ...	1
G. Griffith, c Grundy, b Caffyn............... 3	— not out	11
W. Mortlock, c Lillywhite, b Jackson 3	— b Caffyn	4
G. Anderson, not out 17	— st Lockyer, b Jackson ...	38
W. P. Lockart, Esq., st Lockyer, b Jackson........ 0	— c Lockyer, b Jackson ...	0
T. Sewell, jun., c Carpenter, b Caffyn........ 1	— c Hayward, b Jackson ...	3
R. C. Tinley, b Jackson......................... 3	— c Lockyer, b Jackson ...	13
E. Willsher, c Caffyn, b Jackson 0	— not out	7
G. Tarrant, c Stephenson, b Jackson 0		
J. Bickley, c Carpenter, b Caffyn............. 6		
Byes, &c. 0	Byes 0, 1 b 4, wides 0..	4
40		**101**

BOWLERS.	Balls.	Runs.		BOWLERS.	Balls.	Runs.
Jackson	72	19		Jackson	82	38
Caffyn	71	21		Caffyn	60	19
				Stephenson	28	17
				Hayward	60	23

"The other" England Eleven winning by three wickets.

Frank Glover was a prime mover in pressing for the formation of a County Club and was first to address the group at the inaugural meeting in 1864. He became the first Hon. Secretary of the Club from 1864-1873.

FRANK GLOVER

Above: The new Old Trafford ground consisted of seven acres of good level ground and the committee received £1,300 compensation to prepare the new site and build a pavilion. The ground was situated in a picturesque environment on the outskirts of Manchester. It included a large bowling green to the right and an excellent quoiting ground. The illustration shows Old Trafford in 1861, the year Abraham Lincoln became President of the United States.

The Manchester Courier reported a meeting to be held at the Queen's Hotel, Manchester on 12th January 1864 to discuss the formation of a County Club. Thirteen Lancashire Cricket Clubs were represented including five Manchester Cricket Club Committee members, the Rowley brothers (Alexander and Edmund), E. Challender, Sam Swire and Frank Glover who was appointed at that meeting, the County's first Hon. Secretary. The Earl of Sefton was elected President.

● *The same year the Chimney Sweep Act forbade the use of children being sent up to clean chimneys.*

Below: The first officers of the Lancashire Club *(left to right)* Frank Glover, Sam Swire, Alexander Rowley, E. Challender and Edmund Rowley.

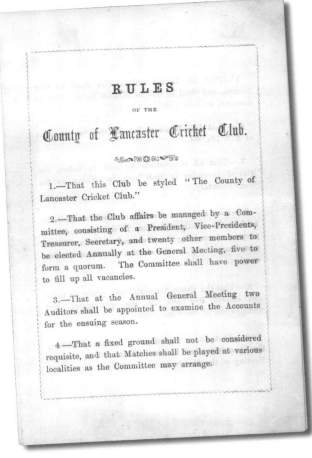

RULES

OF THE

County of Lancaster Cricket Club.

1.—That this Club be styled "The County of Lancaster Cricket Club."

2.—That the Club affairs be managed by a Committee, consisting of a President, Vice-Presidents, Treasurer, Secretary, and twenty other members to be elected Annually at the General Meeting, five to form a quorum. The Committee shall have power to fill up all vacancies.

3.—That at the Annual General Meeting two Auditors shall be appointed to examine the Accounts for the ensuing season.

4.—That a fixed ground shall not be considered requisite, and that Matches shall be played at various localities as the Committee may arrange.

Above: The rules in 1864 indicated that the Club was first called the "County of Lancaster Cricket Club".

Right: The first match under the name of the County of Lancashire was played in 1864 against the popular Birkenhead Park XI at Warrington. The County team consisted of eleven amateurs although in the return game three professionals were employed - William Hickton, Holgate and Nicholls.

LANCASHIRE v. BIRKENHEAD PARK AND GROUND.
At Warrington, June 15th and 16th, 1864.

First Innings — LANCASHIRE.		Second Innings.	
J. Fairclough, Esq., st Darbyshire, b Harvey	4	c Wild, b Darbyshire	0
J. White, Esq., b Harvey	5	b Tennent	7
E. B. Rowley, Esq., b Eaton	29	b Tennent	0
J. Becton, Esq., b Humphrey	0	c Porter, b Tennent	11
B. J. Lawrence, Esq., c Pears, b Humphrey	45	c Humphrey, b Tennent	13
G. H. Grimshaw, Esq., b Wheeler	7	c Wroth, b Darbyshire	16
S. H. Swire, Esq., b Wheeler	0	b Darbyshire	1
J. Rowley, Esq., c Darbyshire, b Tennent	57	c Porter, b Darbyshire	0
F. H. Gossage, Esq., b Humphrey	1	b Tennent	10
W. Robinson, Esq., b Tennent	4	not out	5
T. T. Bellhouse, Esq., not out	0	b Tennent	4
B 7, l b 2, w 7, n b 1	17	B 3, w 5, n b 3	11
	169		**78**

First Innings. — BIRKENHEAD PARK.		Second Innings.	
A. L. Wroth, Esq., b Swire	4		
Wheeler, b Lawrence	20	b E. B. Rowley	31
G. Eaton, Esq., c J. Rowley, b Lawrence	6	not out	13
B. Darbyshire, Esq., c Swire, b Lawrence	8		
W. M. Tennent, Esq., st Fairclough, b Lawrence	11		
Harvey, c J. White, b Lawrence	31	not out	36
W. T. Pears, Esq., c Becton, b Lawrence	16		
A. J. Maclean, Esq., c Swire, b Lawrence	4		
W. Wild, Esq., run out	0		
Humphrey, not out	0		
E. Porter, Esq., c White, b Lawrence	36		
B 3, l b 1, w 3	7	B 1, l b 2, w 7	10
	143		**90**
	Drawn.		

RETURN MATCH, at Birkenhead Park, July 15th and 16th.

First Innings. — LANCASHIRE.		Second Innings.	
J. R. Birkett, Esq., run out	32	c Horner, b Humphrey	17
Hickton, c Bird, b Eaton	80	b Horner	1
F. W. Wright, Esq., b Humphrey	41	st Lockhart, b Horner	11
J. M. Moss, Esq., b Harvey	0	not out	19
S. Rowley, Esq., run out	3	b Harvey	46
A. Appleby, Esq., b Harvey	24	c Wheeler, b Horner	33
J. Rowley, Esq., b Harvey	14	b Harvey	22
B. J. Lawrence, Esq., c Harvey, b Humphrey	7	c Bird, b Humphrey	8
T. Wall, Esq., b Harvey	0	c Lockhart, b Humphrey	8
Holgate, run out	10	st Lockhart, b Horner	0
Nicholls, not out	6	c and b Humphrey	0
B 8, l b 5, w 4	17	L b 3, w 1	4
	234		**174**

BIRKENHEAD PARK AND GROUND.—First Innings.

W. Horner, Esq., run out	17	J. Wheeler, c Appleby, b Lawrence	5
W. M. Tennent, Esq., b Hickton	24	T. Brindley, Esq., c Wright, b Nicholls	36
G. Eaton, Esq., c Nicholls, b Hickton	29	J. Humphrey, c Holgate, b Lawrence	2
B. Darbyshire, Esq., c Moss, b Hickton	37	A. M. Watson, Esq., not out	11
W. P. Lockhart, Esq., b Hickton	10	B 21, w 6, n b 1	28
C. Harvey, c Appleby, b Hickton	1		
E. W. Bird, st Holgate, b Wright	35		**235**
		Drawn.	

The Rowley brothers Alexander and Edmund were prominent in the early years supported by brothers James, Septimus, Arthur, Joseph and Walter. All seven played for the Gentlemen of Lancashire. Edmund Butler Rowley, a solicitor in Manchester usually captained the side when he was able to play. His brother Alexander occasionally took the role.

Extreme left:
Edmund Butler Rowley.
Left: Alexander Rowley.

Left: Member's ticket 1865.

Right: **Bill Hickton** was the first professional to play for Lancashire. In 1870 he took all ten wickets in an innings, 10 for 46, against Hampshire at Old Trafford. It is still a record for the County.

Left: **Fred Reynolds** was a fast round-arm bowler who played for Parr's England XI before joining the Manchester Cricket Club in 1860. He played in Lancashire's initial first class county match against Middlesex at Old Trafford in 1865 taking 6-92 in the return match. After nine years in the side he became the Old Trafford Ground Manager until he retired at 74 years of age.

Above: **Arthur Appleby** was a left-handed fast round-arm bowler and useful bat. He was a mill owner, and business came before cricket on many occasions. Over 21 years as an amateur he played 58 matches from 1866 to 1887. A dangerous bowler, he was chosen to tour North America with Fitzgerald's team in 1872 and played many games for the Gentlemen v the Players.

RULES.

1. That this Club be styled "The County of Lancashire Cricket Club."

2. That the Club affairs be managed by a Committee, consisting of a President, Vice-Presidents, Treasurer, Secretary, and twenty other members, to be elected annually at the General Meeting, five to form a quorum. The Committee shall have power to fill up all vacancies.

3. That at the Annual General Meeting two Auditors shall be appointed to examine the Accounts for the ensuing season.

4. That a fixed ground shall not be considered requisite, and that Matches shall be played at various localities as the Committee may arrange.

5. That the Annual Subscription shall be Five Shillings, and shall be due in advance on the First of January in each year.

6. That Life Members be admitted on payment of £5. 5s.

7. That all resignations be sent in before the 31st of December in each year, in writing to the Secretary.

8. That a General Meeting of the Club shall be held in the month of January in each year, for the purpose of receiving the Treasurer's Accounts for the past season, and for the election of Officers for that ensuing.

9. That the Committee shall have power to make and enforce Bye-Laws for the government and management of the Club.

10. That, on a requisition of Twenty Members, the Committee shall be required to call a General Meeting of the Members.

11. That Birth, or Residence, or place of Business, for three consecutive years, be deemed sufficient qualification for a County Player.

12. That in arranging all Matches it be understood that each side bears its own expenses.

13. That Clubs subscribing to the funds of the Club shall send a representative to the General Meeting of the Club, who shall have the privilege of an ordinary Member.

14. That no alteration be made in the preceding Rules unless at a General Meeting.

A. H. Burgess, Printer, 38, Cannon Street, Manchester.

Right: A copy of the rules of the Lancashire County Cricket Club in 1867.

County of Lancashire Cricket Club

President:
The Right Honorable the EARL of SEFTON.

Vice Presidents:
The Right Honorable the EARL of DERBY.
The Right Honorable the EARL of ELLESMERE.
MARK PHILIPS, Esq.
CHARLES TURNER, Esq., M.P.

Treasurer:
E. CHALLENDER, Esq.

Committee:

APPLEBY, A.	MAKINSON, JOSEPH
BELLHOUSE, T. T.	NICHOLSON, W.
BIRLEY, F. H.	ROWLEY, A. B.
CUNNINGHAM, D.	ROWLEY, E. B.
HORNBY, A. N.	SWIRE, S. H.
LEACH, ROBERT	WALKER, ROGER
LEESE, JOSEPH	WALL, THOMAS, Junr.

Secretary:
R. C. STONEX, 45, Blackfriars Street, Manchester.

Right: Captain E.B. Rowley's letter to Appleby in 1869 appealing for the best amateurs to play for their County: "When Lancashire have such men in the County as yourself and Hornby and they will not play I think it is only fair to expect that the matches will be lost." Dated August 16th 1869.

Clarence Buildings,
South Street, Manchester.
August 6th 1869

Dear Appleby,
When Lancashire have such men in the County as yourself and Hornby and they will not play I think it is only fair to expect that the matches will be lost. At the commencement of the season I was very glad to hear that you and Hornby had arranged to play with Lancashire in the County matches and I certainly understood that Lancashire was to have the expense — but may I ask has this arrangement been kept

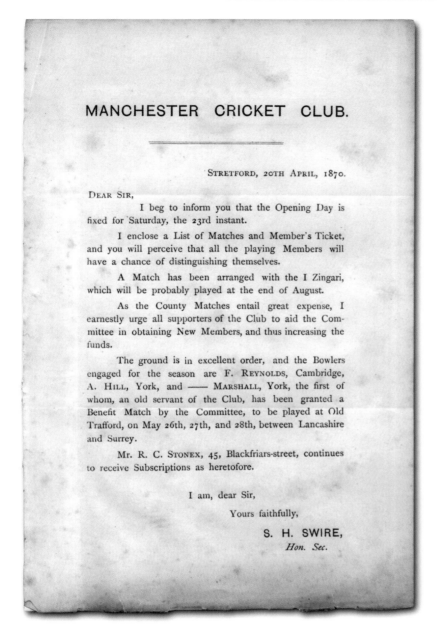

MANCHESTER CRICKET CLUB.

STRETFORD, 20TH APRIL, 1870.

DEAR SIR,

I beg to inform you that the Opening Day is fixed for Saturday, the 23rd instant.

I enclose a List of Matches and Member's Ticket, and you will perceive that all the playing Members will have a chance of distinguishing themselves.

A Match has been arranged with the I Zingari, which will be probably played at the end of August.

As the County Matches entail great expense, I earnestly urge all supporters of the Club to aid the Committee in obtaining New Members, and thus increasing the funds.

The ground is in excellent order, and the Bowlers engaged for the season are F. REYNOLDS, Cambridge, A. HILL, York, and —— MARSHALL, York, the first of whom, an old servant of the Club, has been granted a Benefit Match by the Committee, to be played at Old Trafford, on May 26th, 27th, and 28th, between Lancashire and Surrey.

Mr. R. C. STONEX, 45, Blackfriars-street, continues to receive Subscriptions as heretofore.

I am, dear Sir,

Yours faithfully,

S. H. SWIRE,
Hon. Sec.

Left: A letter from Sam Swire, Hon. Secretary of the Lancashire Cricket Club in 1870, seeks new members to help finance first class matches. Only Fred Reynolds of the bowlers engaged played for the County. The two Yorkshire bowlers listed, Allen Hill, who played for Burnley, went on to take the first English wicket in Test match cricket and Amos Marshall played in the Lancashire leagues.

Below: **Samuel Swire** was Hon. Secretary of Lancashire CCC from 1873 until his death in 1905. He was an amateur cricketer playing in the initial first class game for his County against Middlesex.

Below: Amateurs and professional were separated when dining and travelling in away hotels and in their changing facilities. Amateurs changed in the main Pavilion at Old Trafford whilst professionals were given a "shed" on the west side of the ground. As the professional staff grew in numbers, a new Pavilion was built for them and opened in 1874 on the railway side, directly opposite the main Pavilion. Barlow would appear from this building and Hornby from the main Pavilion opposite and meet on the pitch to open the innings in 1875.

Above: '**Gentlemen of Lancashire**' in 1871.
Back pair (l to r): Harris (umpire), John Leach.
Middle four: Roger Walker, R. Stubbs, A.W. Gardiner, Arthur Appleby.
Seated four: John Hillkirk, William Potter, Edward Porter, John Leese. *Standing right:* Joe Makinson.
On ground left: A.N. Hornby.
Lancashire's amateurs played under the title of 'Gentlemen of Lancashire' in 1871 and a side made up of all professionals was also formed for the first time. This all gentlemen side played Oxford University at Oxford and Cambridge University at Fenners in one trip. The photo was taken at Christchurch Oxford.

⬤ *This year the F.A. Cup was established.*
⬤ *In Africa, Stanley met Livingstone.*

Left: **Will McIntyre** was a fast round arm bowler who took 15 wickets in a match in 1877. His total of 510 wickets averaged only 12.6 runs per wicket.

⬤ *In 1877 the first Wimbledon Championship was held.*

The Hornby Era

T HE most influential figure in cricket, W.G. Grace, revolutionised the game from a village pursuit to a professional sport. Likewise, the strong personality and leadership of A.N. Hornby transformed Lancashire cricket into a new era of prosperity. Born in Blackburn in 1847, he was contemporary with, and the equal of, Lord Harris of Kent, Lord Hawke of Yorkshire and the Grace brothers of Gloucestershire. Hornby was a mighty figure, intolerant of inefficiency and utterly fearless. He went on to serve the County for 50 years as player, Captain, Committee man and President. He was the first Lancashire player to reach 1,000 runs, headed the English averages and led his County to five Championship titles, although three were shared. He was an all-round sportsman, captaining England at cricket and rugby, he played soccer for Blackburn Rovers as well as being an accomplished horseman and pugnacious boxer of some repute. He had the power to infect those around him with enthusiasm and confidence and his charisma drew crowds to watch Lancashire become a major force in the land.

Hornby formed a formidable opening partnership with Richard Barlow, the latter having a stern and implacable defence, a perfect foil for his ebullient superior who stole many a cheeky run. It was a kind of marriage where opposites succeed.

W.G. Grace and his Gloucestershire Championship side were persuaded to visit Old Trafford for the first time in 1878 and over 28,000 spectators came to see the teams. Hornby, who scored a century in the second innings, opened with Barlow, who was last out in the first innings, helped to put Lancashire on top. Gloucestershire held out for a draw but this was a major turning point in the Club's history with its recognition as a major force and popular ground. The Australian touring side came to play Lancashire for the first time later the same year.

Hornby's influence persuaded the Grace brothers to come to Old Trafford.
Above: **A.N. Hornby**   ***Far left:*** **Dr W.G. Grace**
Centre left: **G.F. Grace**   ***Left:*** **Dr E.M. Grace**

The Lancashire Team of 1878 played Gloucestershire the Championship County, watched by over 27,000 over the three-day match. *Front:* R.G. Barlow, A.N. Hornby, E.B. Rowley, A. Appleby, J. Kershaw, R. Pilling.

Back (left to right): A.B. Rowley (President), O.P. Lancashire, A.G. Steel, Rev. V. Royle, A. Watson, W. McIntyre, Fletcher (scorer).

● In 1878 steam road vehicles were limited to 4m.p.h and had to be preceded by a man with a red flag.

Right: Professional **Richard Gorton Barlow** and amateur **Albert Neilson Hornby**.

AT LORD'S

Francis Thompson

It is little I repair to the matches of the Southron folk,
   Though my own red roses there may blow;
It is little I repair to the matches of the Southron folk,
   Though the red roses crest the caps, I know.
For the field is full of shades as I near the shadowy coast,
And a ghostly batsman plays to the bowling of a ghost,
And I look through my tears on a soundless—clapping host
   As the run-stealers flicker to and fro,
      To and fro:—
   O my Hornby and my Barlow long ago !

It is Glo'ster coming North, the irresistible,
   The Shire of the Graces, long ago!
It is Gloucestershire up North, the irresistible,
    And new-risen Lancashire the foe !
A Shire so young that has scarce impressed its traces,
Ah, how shall it stand before all resistless Graces ?
O, little red rose, their bats are as maces
    To beat thee down, this summer long ago !

This day of seventy-eight they are come up North against thee,
   This day of seventy-eight, long ago !
The champion of the centuries, he cometh up against thee,
   With his brethren, every one a famous foe !
The long-whiskered Doctor, that laugheth rules to scorn,
While the bowler, pitched against him, bans the day that he was born:
And G. F. with his science makes the fairest length forlorn;
They are come from the West to work thee woe !

It is little I repair to the matches of the Southron folk,
   Though my own red roses there may blow;
It is little I repair to the matches of the Southron folk,
   Though the red roses crest the caps, I know.
For the field is full of shades as I near the shadowy coast,
And a ghostly batsman plays to the bowling of a ghost,
And I look through my tears on a soundless-clapping host,
   As the run-stealers flicker to and fro,
      To and fro:—
   O my Hornby and my Barlow long ago !

The Lancashire poet **Francis Thompson (below)**, a regular at Old Trafford in his youth, was present at the famous Lancashire v Gloucestershire game. Moving to London, and living in relative poverty, he was invited to Lord's to see a Middlesex v Lancashire game in 1906. When the day came he could not

face it, remembering his momentous days at Old Trafford. The exciting, prolific Hornby and solid Barlow had given him so much pleasure in his youth he could not attend to see new players. He stayed away and composed his famous poem "At Lord's". It is full of nostalgia, touching the innermost soul and evoking images of perfect moments long ago. This mystic Lancashire poet has given the world its greatest cricket poem.

Above: The first official Australian cricket team visited Old Trafford in 1878. There were large crowds in attendance although the match was drawn. Barlow was top scorer for the County and took 5-47 in the Australians' only completed innings.

Right: Lancashire star players, **Dick Barlow** *(left)* opening right hand batsman, successful left hand bowler and excellent fielder at point, and **Richard Pilling**, the best wicket keeper of his day.

In 1879 Lancashire achieved its first championship, shared with Nottinghamshire. When Lancashire could field all their best players, they were a formidable side. Two of the most talented all-rounders played.

Right: **Johnny Briggs**, the most successful all-rounder in the Club's history, made his debut this season.

Allan Steel, a Liverpool barrister, was a brilliant all-rounder, perhaps the most talented of all players but he could not find time to play regularly. He chose the important matches where large crowds, six deep, lined the ground.

CRICKET!

GRAND MATCH,

FOR THE BENEFIT OF J. C SHAW,

(OF NOTTINGHAM),

Professional of the East Lancashire Cricket Club.

LANCASHIRE COUNTY TEAM
v
18 OF EAST LANCASHIRE.

THIS MATCH WILL TAKE PLACE

On FRIDAY & SATURDAY, Aug. 8th & 9th, 1879
ON THE ALEXANDRA MEADOWS,

Adjoining the Corporation Park, Blackburn

LANCASHIRE COUNTY TEAM:

Mr. A. N. Hornby	Mr. E. B. Rowley	R. G. Barlow.	W. Mc.Intyre.
„ A. Appleby.	„ J. E. Kershaw	J. Briggs.	R. Pilling.
„ V. Royle	„ A. G. Steel.	A. Watson.	

THE EIGHTEEN WILL BE SELECTED FROM THE FOLLOWING:

Mr. A. Bertwistle	Mr. C. Coward.	Mr. B. Harwood.	Mr. I. Smith.	Mr. W. Ward.
„ J. S. Bland,	„ F. Coward.	„ T. Houlker.	„ S. J. Sparrow.	„ J. Wolstenholme.
„ T. Branch.	„ T. Eastwood.	„ J. Ingham.	„ W. Standen.	J. C. Shaw.
„ W. H. Briggs.	„ H. Greenwood.	„ F. Isherwood.	„ G Walsh	J. Crossland.
„ W. Burrows.	„ F. Hargreaves.	„ J. Riley.	„ J. Walsh.	G. Nash.
		„ J. Rutherford		

WICKETS PITCHED PUNCTUALLY AT ELEVEN O'CLOCK EACH DAY.

ADMISSION: NORTH END, ONE SHILLING; SOUTH END, SIXPENCE

An early poster showing the Alexander Meadows, Blackburn, ground in 1879.

● *In South Africa the same year, over 3,000 Zulu warriors attacked a British garrison of 80 fit men and Rorke's Drift was defended successfully.*

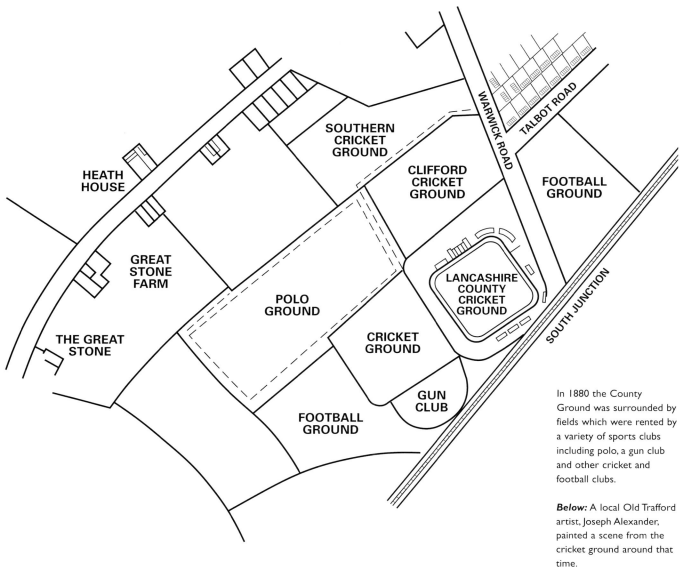

In 1880 the County Ground was surrounded by fields which were rented by a variety of sports clubs including polo, a gun club and other cricket and football clubs.

Below: A local Old Trafford artist, Joseph Alexander, painted a scene from the cricket ground around that time.

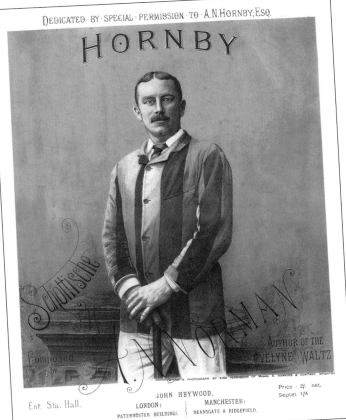

Above: 1880 Team - *Back (left to right):* Umpire, C.G. Hulton, Arthur Appleby, Alex Watson, G. Nash.
Seated: Richard Pilling, Walter Robinson, Edmund Rowley, Albert Hornby, Vernon Royle, Oswald Lancashire.
Front: Richard Barlow.

In 1880 Hornby was asked to captain the County Club. He influenced the decision to amalgamate the Manchester and County clubs. On 24th March 1880 a group of representatives agreed that the new name should be Lancashire County and Manchester Cricket Club. This would remain until 1957. Humphrey De Trafford, the landlord of the ground, was made President, Sam Swire was elected Hon. Secretary and James MacLaren Treasurer. The new Committee was decided by ballot.

● *This year flogging was abolished in the military services and education for children up to the age of 12 years became compulsory.*

Left: Albert Neilson Hornby was held in great respect by the public at large and a piano piece titled Hornby Schottische, by the successful song writer A.N. Norman, was published in the 1880s.

Richard Gorton Barlow

Richard Gorton Barlow was born near Bolton in 1850 and became the first great Lancashire professional. As an outstanding all-rounder he opened the batting and bowling for his County and for England, representing his country on three tours to Australia.

Right: Erected in his back garden near Old Trafford was a cricket net for practice and coaching.

Below right: Barlow was an outstanding sportsman. He won prizes in athletics as a sprinter and hurdler, played football for his county and, as an FA referee, he officiated at the Preston cup-tie when North End defeated Hyde 26-0, a record unlikely to be beaten.

Below: **Barlow** was a first class umpire for 21 years and the first professional player to stand in a Test Match.

In 1884, the North of England team played the Australians on a poor wicket at Trent Bridge. Barlow scored a century and took 10 wickets in the match. Murdoch, the Australian captain was so impressed with Barlow's performance he approached him leaving the field and said "I take my cap off to you" and presented it to Barlow. It became headlines in the press and the saying "I take my hat off to you" comes from this incident.

Right: Murdoch's cap presented to Barlow - the source of the famous saying.

Above: This most interesting cricketer designed his own gravestone. It is a representation of a bat falling to the ground in front of a wicket, broken by a ball and titled "BOWLED AT LAST" This grave is in Leyton Cemetery near Blackpool.

Above: A similar gravestone for Hornby in Acton Churchyard, near Nantwich.

Hornby's leadership brought the Lancashire side to their first outright Championship in 1881. The side won ten of their 13 matches with the other three drawn. Hornby scored over 1,000 runs this season averaging over 50. Allan Steel averaged over 50 and took 42 wickets in only five games. Dick Barlow scored over 500 runs and took 68 wickets.

Below: 1881 Team - *Back (left to right):* G. Nash, J. Crossland, J. Smith (Umpire), R. Pilling, A. Watson.
Middle: A.G. Steel, Rev V.K. Royle, A.N. Hornby, A. Appleby.
Front: W. Robinson, R.G. Barlow, O.P. Lancashire, J. Briggs.

● *In this year the New Zealand settlers made peace with the Maoris and in the USA President Garfield was assassinated after four months in office. Queen Victoria's favourite Prime Minister Disraeli died.*

Above: In 1881 the Pavilion was extended to accommodate the professionals' changing room. They no longer had to walk to the wicket from the opposite side of the ground. The professionals and amateurs had separate dressing rooms, dining facilities, travelling and hotel arrangements. Alex Watson was given accommodation in the Pavilion as the new groundsman. There was also a new Committee Room and Telegraph Office. A train stopped at the cricket ground platform.

Left: The Aigburth ground was opened with a match against Cambridge University which included three Lancashire players, Allan Steel, Oswald Lancashire and John Napier. The new wicket broke up towards the end of the game so no County game was played at Liverpool that season.

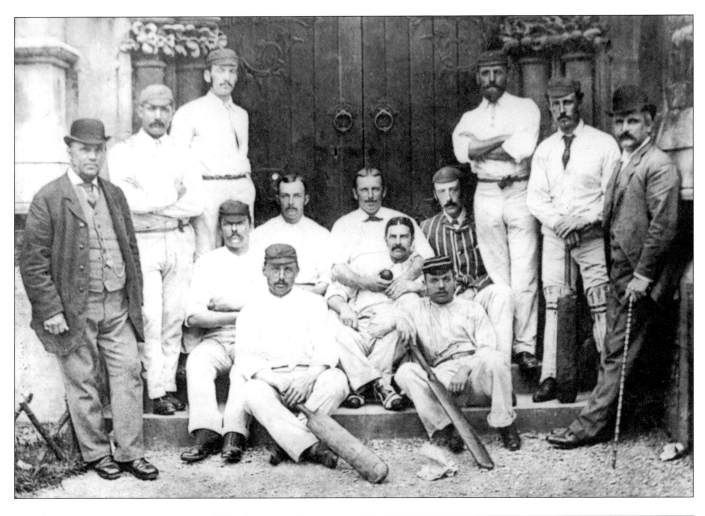

Lancashire again shared the Championship in 1882 with Nottinghamshire. This team beat Surrey by an innings in their last game of the season at The Oval in August. The crowd thought that John Crossland's action was dubious and shouted at the umpire to ban him from bowling. The fast bowler took 6-30 in the first innings and 5-49 in the second, ten of the batsmen clean-bowled. Crossland was never no-balled by any first class umpire in his playing career. He worked down the pit at Clayton-le-Woods in the winter months.

Above: 1882 team - *Standing (left to right):* Rowbotham, G. Nash, Richard Pilling,
Richard Barlow, Alex Watson, James MacLaren.
Seated: John Crossland, C. Haigh, A.N. Hornby,
Vernon Royce, F. Taylor (blazer).
Front: W. Robinson, Johnny Briggs.

Left: **John Crossland**.

Right: **Rev Vernon Royle**
was a useful amateur all-rounder, particularly an outstanding cover point fielder. He played in one Test match in Australia in 1879. After ordination Vernon Royle became the head of a private school in Stanmore Park, Middlesex. He died whilst President of the club in 1929.

Below: Member's ticket for 1882. It was made of leather enclosing the fixtures for the season.

Old Trafford had gone through many physical changes in 1883. Money had been spent on stands, covered and uncovered, dining rooms and ground drainage. The club had 1,237 members and Lord Harris described the ground as the best in the country. A local newspaper reported that the lunch was good and plentiful and waiters were attentive. There were telegraphs, telephones, blackboards for communications and uniformed men to help the public.

Above: 1883 team
Back (left to right): A. Watson, J. Crossland, R. Pilling, W. Robinson, G. Nash.
Middle: H.B. Steel, A.N. Hornby, S.M. Crosfield, E. Roper.
Front: R.G. Barlow, J. Briggs, Cornelius Coward.

A Test match was played at Old Trafford in 1884, the second ground in the country after The Oval and before Lord's. The England side included four Lancashire players, Hornby who was captain, Dick Barlow, Allan Steel and Richard Pilling.

Below: Lancashire also played the Australians, thousands turning up to watch the game.

Richard Pilling was Lancashire's keeper from 1877-89 and regarded widely as the best in the country. He played eight Test matches against Australia, his career being cut short by his early death at 35 years.

Above: Lady's season ticket for 1884 in leather.

Top left: **Alex Watson** was an accurate off spinner taking over 1300 wickets averaging 13.3. He played 283 matches for Lancashire between 1871-93 as a professional and on retirement started a successful sports shop in Manchester.

Left: **Johnny Briggs** was a cheerful, popular player only 5ft 5ins in height and was 16 years of age when he first played for Lancashire. He appeared in 33 Test matches over 16 seasons, touring Australia six times. He is the only cricketer to have taken a Test hat-trick and scored a century for England. Briggs was an excellent fielder at cover point, a hard-hitting batsman and a most successful left arm spin bowler. In 1885 he took 9-29 against Derbyshire and went on to take over 2,000 first class wickets and score over 14,000 runs.

Below: **George Kemp** was an all round sportsman excelling at tennis, athletics and cricket at Cambridge and scoring a century in his first Roses match in 1885. He became Lord Rochdale in 1913.

Left: The famous stained glass window portrays **A N Hornby**, wicket keeper **Richard Pilling** and at the crease **Richard Barlow**. All three Lancashire players represented England in the first Test played at Old Trafford in 1884, Hornby captaining the side. The background shows the County Ground with the Old Pavilion behind Hornby and the new Ladies Pavilion behind Barlow. The window was given to Barlow by the Lancashire County Cricket Club for helping to bring back the Ashes from Australia in 1887. It was brought back to Old Trafford in the 1980s and can be seen in the Pavilion long room.

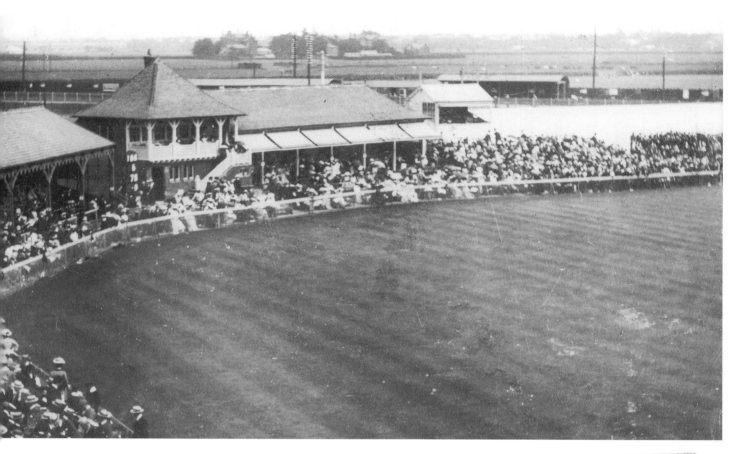

Above: In the centre of the photo is the Ladies Pavilion built in 1885 with a structure two stories high to accommodate a cloak and tea room. The covered stand extension provided seating for 300 ladies.

Below: The members' area was extended also.

⬤ *This year General Gordon was killed two days before the relief expedition arrived in the Sudan.*

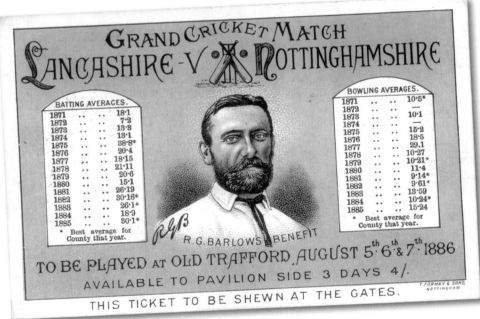

GRAND CRICKET MATCH
LANCASHIRE - V - NOTTINGHAMSHIRE

BATTING AVERAGES.				
1871	..	..	18·1
1872	..	..	7·2
1873	..	..	13·3
1874	..	..	13·1
1875	..	..	38·8*
1876	..	..	20·4
1877	..	..	18·15
1878	..	..	21·11
1879	..	..	20·6
1880	..	..	15·1
1881	..	..	26·19
1882	..	..	30·16*
1883	..	..	26·1*
1884	..	..	18·9
1885	..	..	30·1*

* Best average for County that year.

R.G.B

R.G. BARLOWS BENEFIT

BOWLING AVERAGES.			
1871	..	..	10·5*
1872			
1873	..	..	10·1
1874			—
1875	..	..	15·2
1876	..	..	18·5
1877	..	..	29·1
1878	..	..	10·27
1879	..	..	10·21*
1880	..	..	11·4
1881	..	..	9·14*
1882	..	..	9·61*
1883	..	..	13·59
1884	..	..	10·24*
1885	..	..	15·24

* Best average for County that year.

TO BE PLAYED AT OLD TRAFFORD AUGUST 5th 6th & 7th 1886
AVAILABLE TO PAVILION SIDE 3 DAYS 4/.
THIS TICKET TO BE SHEWN AT THE GATES.

T. FORMAN & SONS, NOTTINGHAM

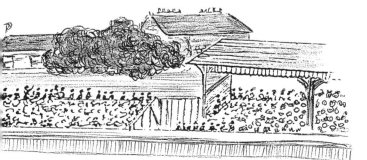

Above: Barlow's benefit ticket, 4 shillings for three days in the Pavilion.

Right: **Allan G. Steel** captained England to victory in each of the three Tests against Australia in 1886, Barlow taking 7-41 and scoring 68 for once out at Old Trafford. Barlow was granted his benefit game against Nottinghamshire at Old Trafford and over 26,000 people paid for admission. Hornby and Barlow scored an opening partnership of 109.

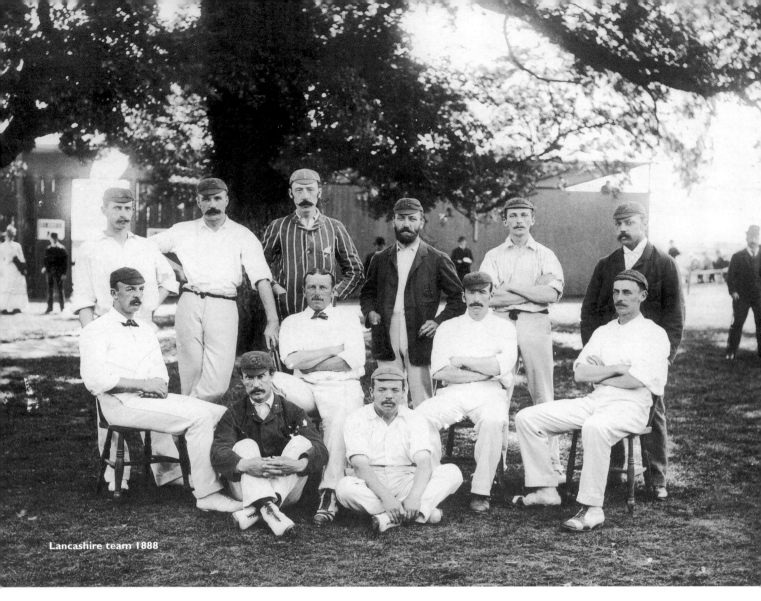

Lancashire team 1888

Australian team 1888

In 1888 a strong Lancashire side beat the Australian team at Old Trafford, Briggs taking 4-34 and 5-15. He took well over 100 wickets in the season as well as scoring most runs for his County. Briggs was one of Wisden's 'chosen' cricketers.

Left: 1888 Lancashire Team.
Back (left to right): G.R. Baker, F.H. Sugg, Mr F. Taylor, R.G. Barlow, Mr E. Steel, G. Yates.
Middle: Mr S.M. Crosfield, Mr A.N. Hornby, R. Pilling, Mr J. Eccles.
Front: A. Watson, J. Briggs.

Below left: The Australian Team.
Back (left to right): Ferris, Jarvis, Worrall, Beal (Manager), Blackham, Boyle, Edwards.
Front: Bonner, Turner, MacDonnell (Captain), Trott, Bannerman.

Above: Railings were placed all round the ground to stop the huge crowds spilling onto the field.

Below: **Rev. John Russell Napier** was a fast bowler from Preston. He played only two games for his County in 1888. His first was against Australia who needed only 90 to win. Napier took 3-54 and 4-48 helping Lancashire to victory by 23 runs. In his second match against Yorkshire he took four wickets in 14 balls without conceding a run. His church work took priority and he never played again.

Left: Advert for Barlow's shop in Manchester.

● The first edition of the Financial Times was issued and the Football League was founded this year. The Coal Mines Act of 1888 stated that no boy under 13 years should work underground. The daily newspapers were full of Jack the Ripper's murders.

FOR FIRST-CLASS GOODS CHEAPEST HOUSE IN

THE TRADE. PRICE LIST POST FREE.

BARLOW'S DURABLE MATCH

BARLOW'S DURABLE MATCH

R. G. BARLOW BRITISH SPORTS DEPOT. VICTORIA STATION APPROACH MANCHESTER.

REGISTERED

Lancashire County Cricket & Athletic Depot.

R. G. BARLOW

(Member of Anglo-Australian, All-England, and Lancashire County Elevens)

HAS now on hand at his NEW ESTABLISHMENT a first-class Stock of WELL-SEASONED BATS, &c.

Note the Prices of BARLOW's Special

ALL-CANE HANDLE BATS -	6/6	Usually sold at	9/6
BARLOW'S ALL-CANE HANDLE Bats warranted superior, no better make	9/6	Usually sold at	12/6
COBBETT'S BEST MATCH BATS -	12/6	Usually sold at	15/6
BARLOW'S CROWN BALL - -	5/6	Per Doz.	60/-
BARLOW'S TREBLE-SEAMED MATCH BALLS, warranted - -	4/-	Usually sold at	5/-

Per Doz., 44/-

BARLOW'S PATENT DURABLE SPIKES — Per Set. 9d.

"The Young Cricketer's Instructor."—Barlow on Batting, Bowling, and Fielding, and Pilling on Wicket Keeping. Acknowledged to be the best book of its kind ever published. Price Sixpence, post-free.

Barlow's Kangaroo Spring Bats are the best known for driving and off-hitting. Made with a powerful spring action which never jars. Try one and if not liked will be exchanged.

Prices—The "CLUB KANGAROO" -	-	13/6
The "SPECIAL KANGAROO" -	-	16/6

(Very light and old seasoned, for private use).

RICE'S Unique Flexible Handle Bat - - 17/6

Note Address— **R. G. BARLOW,**

7, Victoria Station Approach, Manchester.

Right: In 1888 **Samuel Swire** was presented with a large silver tray for his 25 years as Hon. Secretary of the Manchester Cricket Club. Swire was a major participant in the formation of the Lancashire Club, playing in the first game and taking over as Hon. Secretary of the LCCC from Frank Glover in 1873.

Above: A fine portrait in oils of Sam Swire, the patriarch of Lancashire cricket, hangs in the long room in the Pavilion where he stares out on to the ground which he did so much to develop.

Below: Charles Bayley (standing) was the Chairman of the Swire Testimonial Fund which included Frank Glover as Hon. Secretary, R. Gorton, Ted Roper who played as an amateur, A.N. Hornby captain of the side, Alex Rowley, E. Challender and the Mayor of Salford.

The MacLaren Era

A RCHIE MacLAREN played for his County in 1890, four years later he became captain and he was called up to play for England the following year. In his prime he was regarded as the finest batsman in England, a noble and majestic player. Cardus wrote "His cricket belonged in the golden age of the game, to the spacious and opulent England of his day!"

He opened the batting for some years with Reggie Spooner, J.T. Tyldesley coming in at number three. Albert Ward and Frank Sugg added to the team's strong batting. A balanced bowling attack included Johnny Briggs, Arthur Mold and Alec Watson later joined by prominent bowlers Harry Dean, Walter Brearley and the great S.F. Barnes.

Lancashire were runners-up in the Championship five times in seven years before 1897 when they were outright champions again. The number of amateurs in the side had dropped to an average of two per game and the professional playing staff grew to over 20 by the end of the century. Soon afterwards the amateurs and professionals entered the field through the same gate.

Left: **Archie MacLaren** made an immediate impact scoring a century on his debut in 1890 at the age of 18 years. He was Harrow-educated but born only two miles from Old Trafford where he played until 1914. MacLaren was a stylish opening batsman, a strong charismatic leader, and captain of Lancashire and England.

Left: **Arthur Kemble** as an amateur kept wicket occasionally for Lancashire between 1885-94 and at times captained the side. He was a solicitor in Liverpool and played rugby for England.

Below left: The newspaper cartoon suggested the August weather at Old Trafford was very wet, but all three first class matches that month in 1892 were completed. Watched by a daily crowd of 20,000, Lancashire beat Yorkshire by an innings, Briggs scoring a century and taking 13 wickets in the match. The team then beat Somerset in a day by eight wickets, Briggs taking 12 wickets, and then finally beat Nottinghamshire by an innings.

Below: **Sydney Crosfield** was joint captain with Archie MacLaren in 1892-93. The former was a solicitor by profession and an excellent marksman, winning prizes for shooting.

The crowd outside the Entrance to the Old Trafford Ground, on Monday last.

FRANK SUGG LTD LORD ST LIVERPOOL
Branches, 54 Snig Hill Sheffield   8 Queen St Cardiff
4 New Station St Leeds

ADMISSION 6° EACH
EVERY ONE ENTERING
TAKES HIS OWN RISK
OF THE WEATHER
NO MONEY
RETURNED

The famous
BOUNDARIE, JESSOP &
INVINSA CRICKET BATS.

Above: **Frank Sugg** was a hard hitting batsman with a good eye. He played 235 matches for Lancashire and two Test matches for England in 1888. As an all-round sportsman he played football for Bolton Wanderers, Burnley, Sheffield Wednesday and Derby County. His sports shops are still in business today.

Left: Advert for Sugg's shop in Liverpool.

● *In 1893 the Manchester Ship Canal was completed and the following year Blackpool Tower was opened.*

In 1895 five more counties joined the Championship league; Derbyshire, Essex, Leicestershire, Warwickshire and Hampshire. At the beginning of the season a new Pavilion was opened costing nearly £12,000. It was a grand stone Victorian building with great character - second only to the larger Pavilion at Lord's. Three bathrooms were built for the amateurs and one for the professionals even though there were more of the latter. Extended seating was provided in front as the new Pavilion was set further back from the field. The same architect was employed to build the new Pavilion at The Oval a few years later.

● *This year Rhodesia was founded by Ceceil Rhodes.*

Above: Old Trafford in 1895.

Below right: 1895 Lancashire Team -
Back (left to right): A.W. Mold, A.G. Paul, Lunt (Scorer), G.R. Baker, A.P. Smith.
Middle: A. Ward, S.M. Tindall, A.C. MacLaren (C), G.R. Bardswell, F.H. Sugg.
Front: J. Briggs, C. Smith, A. Tinsley.

In 1895 Archie MacLaren became captain of Lancashire although he was unable to play in all the matches. He did captain the side against Somerset at Taunton in July and scored a magnificent 424 - the highest individual score - which was a record for 99 years until Brian Lara scored his 500 at Edgbaston in 1994.

Above: The scorecard from the record-breaking game at Taunton in 1895.

Right: A presentation made to Archie MacLaren in recognition of his record score.

Right: Archie MacLaren was captain of Lancashire for 12 seasons, scoring a century on his debut for the county in 1890 at 18 years of age. He became captain at 23 years when he made his highest score of 424 at Taunton. He led England in 22 Tests against Australia, still a record. MacLaren was a tall, powerful, stylish batsman who shared an opening partnership 368 with Reggie Spooner in 1903, still a record for the County. His father was Hon. Treasurer of the club and later Archie became the County coach. His last first class game was for M.C.C. against New Zealand as captain in 1923 when he scored 200 not out at the age of 51 years.

The new Pavilion in 1895.

Lancashire team 1895

Albert Ward played 330 matches for Lancashire, mostly as an opening batsman, scoring nearly 18,000 runs. He played in seven Test matches scoring a century against Australia in Sydney on the 1894-95 tour.

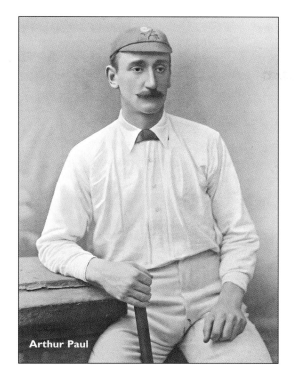

Arthur Paul

Sydney Tindall

Arthur Mold

Above left: **Arthur Paul** became well known for his partnership of 363 with MacLaren at Taunton in 1895. He played rugby for Swinton and was a goalkeeper for Blackburn Rovers. On his retirement in 1900 he became coach at Old Trafford for nearly 30 years.

Left: **Arthur Mold** played 260 matches for Lancashire as a successful fast bowler taking over 1,600 wickets at 15.5. He played three Tests for England in 1893.

Above: **Sydney Tindall**. An amateur batsman in the 1890s, he emigrated to Australia in 1911 and became Secretary of the Melbourne Cricket Club.

In 1896 straw hats were the fashion, The captain, MacLaren, was often unavailable and on occasions the less talented amateurs captained the side even when seasoned professionals such as Albert Ward, Frank Sugg and Johnny Briggs played. Ernest Rowley, son of Edmund, was asked to captain this team at Taunton where Lancashire beat Somerset by 10 wickets. Charles Benton, the only other amateur, was to commit suicide at the age of 50 years.

Left: The Lancashire team pictured at Taunton in 1896
Back (left to right): A.W. Hallam, A.W. Mold,
G.R. Baker, J. Briggs.
Middle: A. Ward, C.H. Benton, Ernest Rowley (Captain),
F.H. Sugg, A.G. Paul.
Front: J.T. Tyldesley, C. Smith, J. I'anson.

Below: A members' ticket from 1896.

Above: **Willis Cuttell.**

Lancashire were runners-up in the championship five times in seven years before 1897 when they were outright champions again, Johnny Briggs, Arthur Mold and Willis Cuttell taking 100 wickets each.

Left: **Arthur Mold** called for dubious action on occasions by one umpire. *RIP* puts his arms in splints.

Right: **Johnny Briggs** - all round entertainer.

Above: **Albert Hallam** played 71 matches for Lancashire as a medium pace bowler taking 100 wickets in 1897. After a back injury he left to join Nottinghamshire where he had further success.

Above: **George Baker** was a fine high order batsman playing 228 matches for Lancashire. He coached at Harrow school when he retired in 1899.

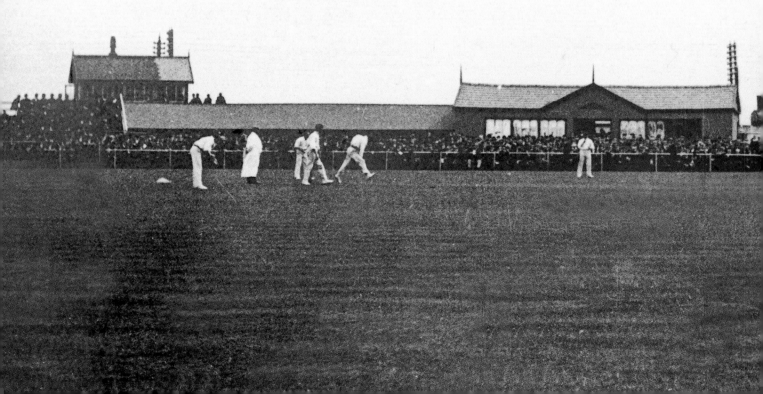

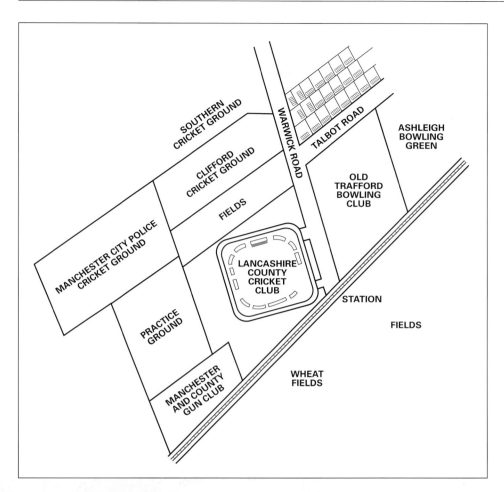

Left: In 1898 the Lancashire Committee decided to purchase the ground and some adjoining land, including the practice field, for £24,732 which put them seriously in the red. They tried to raise the subscription of members from one guinea to two but were unsuccessful. Although it gave the Club financial problems for many years, purchasing the land was one of the wisest decisions the Committee made.

Below: The Lancashire v Yorkshire game at Old Trafford in 1897. The train awaits passengers as the last two Yorkshire batsmen are in. Lord Hawke faces Willis Cuttell at 70 for 9. The other wicket taker Johnny Briggs is at cover point. In the middle of the photograph is the professionals' pavilion, used until 1881. It is on the opposite side of the ground to the main pavilion. The press box is in the centre of the photograph. The scorers sit in the smaller hut to the right. The scoreboard is in between. To the right of the scorer's hut is a box indicating the batsmen at the wicket and the bowlers bowling, by the numbers on the scorecard. Lord Hawke is batting.

Right: Willis Cuttell was the first Lancashire cricketer to achieve the double of 100 wickets and 1,000 runs in a season in 1898. He was chosen to play for England in the first Test series against South Africa the following winter. Cuttell played League cricket with Nelson where he helped them win their first championship in 1892. He was a spin bowler turning the ball both ways, a hard hitting batsman and excellent fielder.

Above: The watch presented to Cuttell for his double achievement.

Four major, influential players made their debut in 1899.

Jack Sharp, who was professional with Leyland, played over 500 matches for Lancashire. Turning amateur in 1919 he was captain from 1923-5. He played soccer for Aston Villa and later Everton, winning a cup final medal with them and going on to play for England at cricket and football.

Facing page (top): In the Test match at Old Trafford in 1899, 28,000 people watched the first day's play. New temporary stands had to be erected. W.G. Grace and Prince Ranjitsinhji drew the crowds as star players. They are pictured here in the Trent Bridge Test that year against the Australians along with R.G. Barlow who was the umpire.

Facing page (bottom left): **Albert Henry Hornby**, son of A.N., captained the County from 1908-1914. He made his first class debut for Cambridge University in 1898 and became a sound positive batsman and brilliant fielder.

Facing page (bottom right): **Reggie Spooner** was the most graceful amateur batsman with excellent timing and was one of the best players of his day. He played for England when he could, turning down the captaincy for the 1920-21 series to Australia. He fought in the Boer war from 1900-02 but played 170 matches for his County 1899-1921.

S.F. Barnes is thought by many to be the most effective bowler in the history of the game world wide. He was picked for England as an unknown by MacLaren and taken to Australia. He took 49 wickets, missing the 5th Test in South Africa, still a record for the series. Sydney Barnes played for Lancashire 1899-1903, preferring to play the less demanding league cricket where he took 100 wickets regularly every season, even in his 50's. He signed his last professional contract at 65 years.

Right: Jack Sharp.

Far right: **Sydney Barnes** (on the left) with friend Joe Allen.

Left: A game between Surrey and Lancashire at The Oval in 1900. Tom Richardson bowls to Albert Ward who scored over 1,500 runs in the season. Jim Hallows is at the non-striker's end in the floppy white hat.

Below left: **Alex Eccles** was a stylish batsman who was awarded three Oxford Blues for cricket 1897-99. He was an amateur who occasionally captained the side, representing Lancashire in 123 matches.

Below right: **Gerald Bardswell**, an amateur from Liverpool, was joint captain with Archie MacLaren in 1899. He was an Oxford Blue, captaining the side in 1897. Gerry Bardswell bowled medium pace early in his career, later developing his batting and becoming a brilliant slip fielder.

Right: In 1900 **Johnny Briggs** (seen standing in the delightful family picture on the right) took all ten wickets in an innings at Old Trafford. His infectious enthusiasm made him the most popular of players. He had suffered an epileptic fit during the Headingley Test match the previous year and spent the winter in Cheadle Royal Hospital. The season of 1900 was his last; he returned to Cheadle the following year where he died aged 39 years. Many thousands attended his funeral. Johnny's father was a league professional with Widnes C.C. and his brother Joe (seated on the right) played for Nottinghamshire.

Alex Eccles

Gerald Bardswell

Right: In 1901 the officials and members of the club presented A.N. Hornby with a large portrait of himself in his later playing days. It hangs in the Pavilion Long Room. His last innings was two years earlier when he scored 53 against Leicestershire.

Below: **Harold Garnett** was an amateur left hand bat and wicket-keeper, who went to Australia with MacLaren, J.T. Tyldesley and S.F. Barnes in 1901, but did not play in a Test match. Business interests limited his appearances but he played 144 matches for Lancashire between 1899-1914 and kept wicket for the Gentlemen v Players in his last year.

● *In 1901 Marconi sent the first transatlantic radio signal from Cornwall to Newfoundland.*

The 1902 Test match at Old Trafford was one of the most exciting in the history of cricket. The famous Australian Victor Trumper scored a century before lunch. The England team, led by MacLaren and widely regarded as the best England team ever, should have won the game but Fred Tate, father of Maurice, dropped a vital catch. In the last innings England needed only four runs to win when Tate was bowled.

Above: Abel and Palairet opening for England at Old Trafford.

Right: **Victor Trumper.**

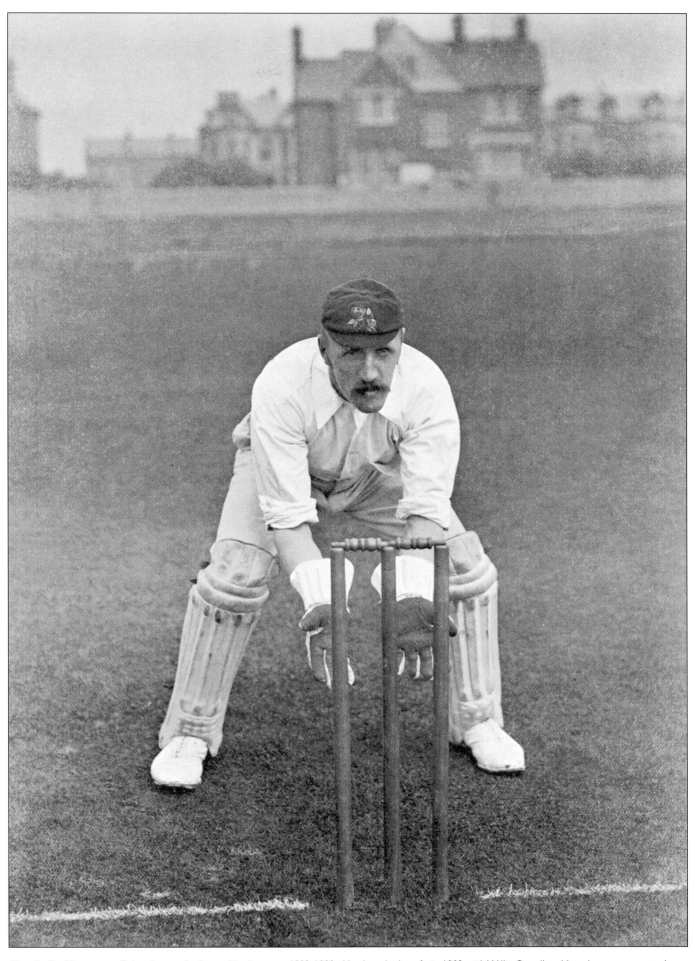

Charlie Smith was an efficient keeper for Lancashire between 1893-1902. He shared a benefit in 1903 with Willis Cuttell and bought a newsagents shop on retirement.

Above: Liverpool born amateur **William Findlay** made his debut for Lancashire in 1902 as a wicket keeper. He was also captain of Oxford and later became secretary of MCC and its President in 1951-52.

Above: Lancashire professionals in 1903 *(left to right):* J.T. Tyldesley, Willis Cuttell, Jimmy Heap, Alex Kermode and Arthur Sladen.

Right: Albert Knight, the Leicestershire batsman, Len Braund the Somerset all-rounder and Lancashire's **J.T. Tyldesley** (far right) aboard the SS Orontes on their way with the MCC team to Australia 1903.

● *In 1903 the top speed limit for the motor car was 20m.p.h.*

● *Women suffragettes were protesting against Parliament at being denied the vote.*

Left: In 1903, **Reggie Spooner** and **Archie MacLaren** scored a record opening partnership at Liverpool of 368 against Gloucestershire, still a record for the county.

In 1904 Lancashire won the Championship again with all-rounder Jimmy Hallows, uncle of Charlie, completing the double. He was a similar cricketer to Briggs, a slow left arm spinner, hard hitter and suffered epileptic fits, dying young at 36 years.

Left: **Jimmy Hallows.**

Below: Lancashire's professionals in 1904 *(left to right):* J.S. Heap, W.R. Cuttell, A.R. Sladen, J.T. Tyldesley, J. Hallows, A. Kermode, J. Sharp.

Above: Lancashire - County Champions 1904.
Back (left to right): J. Sharp, W.R. Cuttell, W. Worsley, W. Findlay, A. Kermode, L.O.S. Poidevin, J. Hallows, W. Brearley, J.S. Heap. *Front:* J.T. Tyldesley, A.N. Hornby, A.C. MacLaren, R.H. Spooner, H.G. Garnett.

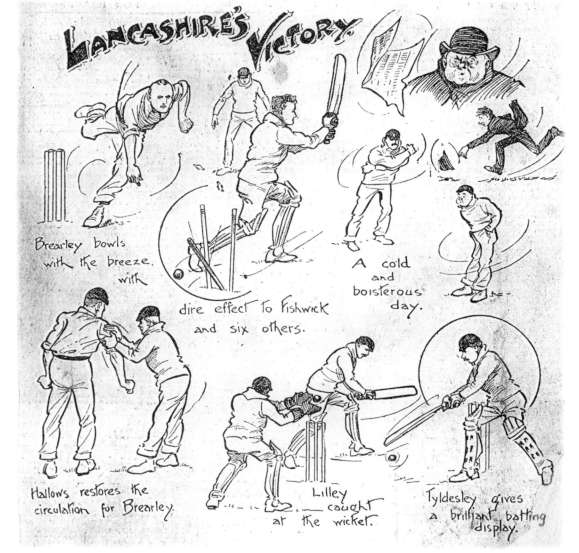

Right: On a cold and windy morning in early May, Lancashire started the 1904 season with a win against Warwickshire, Walter Brearley taking 11 wickets in the match. The team carried on to be unbeaten all season.

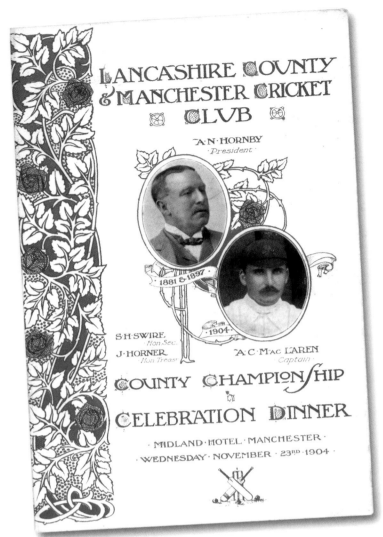

Above: This newspaper cutting demonstrates the influence A.N. Hornby had over the selection committee in 1905.

Left: 1904 Celebration Dinner menu.

Below: Lancashire v Yorkshire was always a well-attended game on the Bank Holiday. A drawn game at Old Trafford in 1904 saw Brearley take six wickets in the first innings, Rhodes and Haigh putting on 150 for the 9th wicket for Yorkshire.

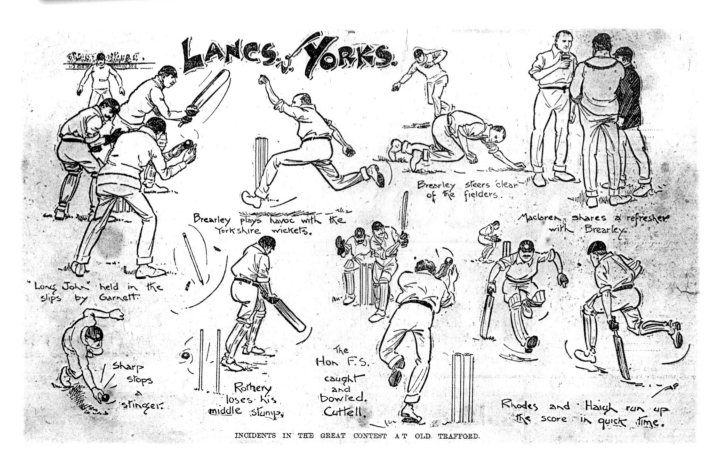

Above: 1905 Team - *Back (left to right):* J. Hallows, W. Findlay, A. Kermode, W. Worsley, J. Sharp, J.T. Tyldesley.
Middle: W. Brearley, L.O.S. Poidevin, A.C. MacLaren, H.G. Garnett, A.H. Hornby. *Front:* G. Radcliffe, J.S. Heap.

Lancashire were runners-up in 1905 and well beaten by the Australian team in May. Walter Brearley took 7-115 for Lancashire. He was a fast amateur bowler taking 17 wickets in a match against Somerset later in the season, the first Lancastrian to take that number, including four wickets in four balls. He should have played more than four Tests but had frequent disputes with the authorities.

● *Frederick Henry Royce met Charles Rolls in Manchester Midland Hotel in 1905 and the Rolls-Royce company was formed, the first cars costing £395.*

Right: Large crowds were watching Lancashire league cricket in 1904. There was a professional, competitive approach to league cricket which helped develop players for the County side. Here Church is playing Accrington.

J.T. Tyldesley made 295 not out against Kent at Old Trafford in 1906.
A young left-hander called Frank Woolley was making his debut for the opposition and he remembered J.T's innings all his life. Tyldesley had a record benefit match against Yorkshire when 4,000 people were turned away, unable to join the 26,000 already in the ground. He was rewarded with a bumper sum of £3,111.
.

J.T. played 507 matches for Lancashire. An attacking powerful driver, good on bad wickets, he is thought by many to be Lancashire's best ever batsman.

Above: Kent batting, Dillon facing Frank Harry.

Right: J.T.'s 1906 benefit card

Below: **'John Tommy' Tyldesley.**

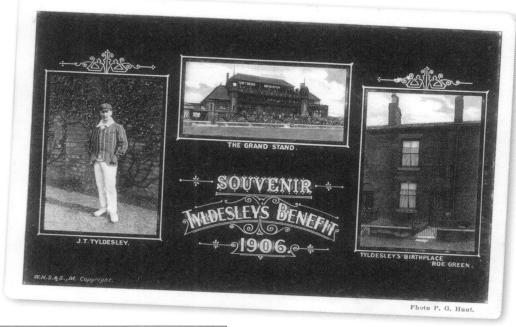

THE GRAND STAND.

SOUVENIR
TYLDESLEY'S BENEFIT
1906

J.T. TYLDESLEY.

TYLDESLEY'S BIRTHPLACE
ROE GREEN.

W.H.S.&S.,M. Copyright.

Photo P. G. Hunt.

Archie MacLaren took his team home after the second day of the Middlesex match at Lord's in 1907. No play was possible on a wet pitch and the umpires pulled up stumps at almost 5p.m. Angry spectators trampled on the wicket and MacLaren decided he could not continue the game. There was some disagreement from the opposition.

Right: 1907 Lancashire Team
Back (left to right): F. Harry, J. Sharp, A. Kermode, W. Huddleston, L.W. Cook, J.W.H. Makepeace.
Middle: H.D. Stanning, L.O.S. Poidevin, A.C. MacLaren, A.H. Hornby, J.T. Tyldesley.
Front: W. Worsley, MacLaren Jnr, H. Dean.

The ground staff were taken on an annual picnic paid for by the club. In 1906 it had developed into lunch and tea at the Royal Hotel in Blackpool.

Below: Lancashire played at Blackpool for the first time in 1906.

In 1908 there were two outstanding bowlers. **Walter Brearley** topped the averages with 148 wickets and **Harry Dean** captured 124. Dean, far right on the back row, was a fast left arm bowler from Burnley who could swing the ball late. He played in three Tests for England. **Bill Huddleston**, top left, was a Lancashire born accurate off-break bowler who supported the opening pair successfully.

J. T. Tyldesley, front right, had a magnificent season with the bat scoring over 2,000 runs, **Jack Sharp**, front left, and **Alfred Hartley**, seated behind Tyldesley, reached 1,000 each. Hartley's father had played for the county as wicket keeper before working in the USA where Alfred was born. The son was a solid opening batsman with a sound defence. He was killed in action in 1918 aged 39 years.

The middle row on this team photograph were all distinguished amateurs.

Left: 1908 Team - *Back (left to right):* W. Huddleston, R. Whitehead, W. Phillips, F. Harry, H. Dean.
Middle: L.O.S. Poidevin, A.C. MacLaren, A.H. Hornby, A. Hartley, A.F. Spooner.
Front: J. Sharp, J.T. Tyldesley.

⬤ *In 1908 Baden Powell founded the Boy Scouts Movement.*

Right: Five Lancashire amateurs in 1908. At the back left is the stylish batsman Reggie Spooner and with him is the hard-hitting Ken Macleod. Seated left to right are captain A.H.Hornby, Archie MacLaren and Leslie Poidevin, who came from Australia to qualify as a doctor.

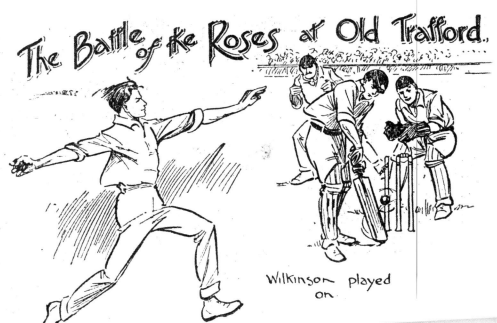

The Battle of the Roses at Old Trafford.

Wilkinson played on

K G Macleod showed his bowling ability.

Left: Amateur all-rounder **Ken Macleod** also excelled in athletics at Cambridge where he gained cricket and rugby Blues, representing Scotland ten times as a wing three-quarter.

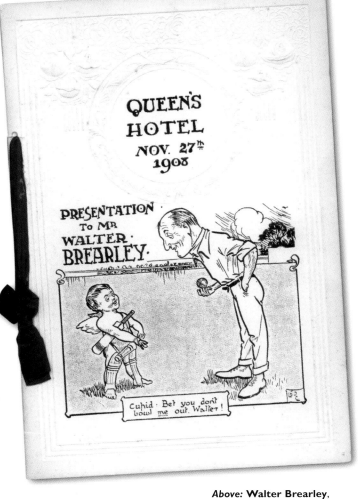

QUEEN'S HOTEL NOV. 27TH 1908

PRESENTATION TO MR WALTER BREARLEY

Cupid · Bet you don't bowl me out, Walter!

Above: **Walter Brearley**, the amateur fast bowler from Bolton, married the daughter of an hotelier in the Lake District in 1908 and the club presented him with a writing cabinet at a dinner at the Queen's Hotel, the venue of the formation of the club.

Left: **Walter Brearley** with **Warwick Armstrong**, the Australian captain, in 1920-21.

Walter Brearley, the Lancashire fast bowler, is the man who is expected to play a prominent part in the Test Matches.

A PEEP INTO HISTORY.

Sir Walter Raleigh (Mr. Brearley) assisting in the stately progress of Queen Elizabeth (Mr. Hornby) to the Championship.

Above left: The press saw **Walter Brearley** as the danger man against Australia in the 1909 Test matches.

Above right: A cartoon in the *Manchester Evening News*, June 26th 1909, predicts Walter Brearley's bowling will help Lancashire win the Championship. He took well over 100 wickets in the season but they finished runners-up to Kent.

Right: **Jack Sharp** taking **J. T. Tyldesley** for a ride in his newly-purchased machine.

Right: In the Triangular Tests held at Old Trafford on May 28th, 1912, **Jimmy Matthews**, took two hat-tricks on the same day for Australia who beat South Africa.

● *Earlier this year 1,500 people lost their lives after the sinking of the Titanic and Robert Falcon Scott died after reaching the South Pole.*

In 1913 brothers **J.T.** and **Ernest Tyldesley** set up a unique record in one week in June when they each scored a century in the same innings, twice.

Below: 1913 Team *Back (l to r):* Trott (Umpire), W. Huddleston, L.W. Cook, R. Whitehead, E. Tyldesley, J. Sharp, Smith (Scorer). *Middle:* J.T. Tyldesley, R.A. Boddington, A.H. Hornby, K. MacLeod, H. Dean. *Front:* J. Heap, H. Makepeace.

Above: Harry Dean was a left arm medium fast bowler who could swing the ball late. He took 1,300 wickets between 1906 and 1921 playing in three Test matches in 1912. When King George V visited Liverpool in 1913, Dean took 17 wickets for 91 against Yorkshire at Aigburth, still a Lancashire record for match aggregate figures (9-62 & 8-29).

Above: William Huddleston took 100 wickets in 1913 as an off-break bowler but the war interrupted a successful career.

Right: In the 1913-14 South African MCC Tour, **S.F. Barnes** took 49 wickets in four Test matches. In the Johannesburg Test his figures were 17-159 in the match.

Below: In 1914 Lancashire played at six grounds - Liverpool, Whalley, Castleton, Blackpool, Old Trafford and once only at Lancaster (pictured), where they played Warwickshire. The team was Jimmy Heap, Ernest Tyldesley, Bill Huddleston, Ralph Whitehead, Bill Tyldesley, Harry Makepeace, all on the back row.
Seated: Jack Sharp, Harold Barnett, Albert H. Hornby (Capt) J.T. Tyldesley and Harry Dean.

● *Three days after this match war was declared on Germany, However Lancashire carried on playing and fulfilled their programme of matches for the season.*

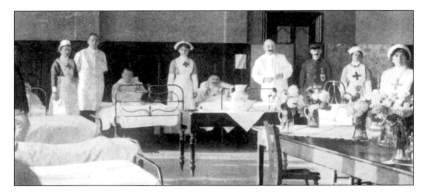

Left: In the winter of 1914, the British Red Cross took over the Pavilion at Old Trafford where 80 sick and wounded men were accommodated. Over the period of the war 1,800 patients were treated.

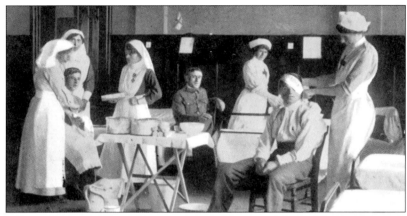

Below: E. Tyldesley, H.G. Garnett, J. Sharp, W. Huddleston and J.T. Tyldesley at Bournemouth, August 1914.

The Successful Twenties

Right: In 1919 cricket was resumed and **Myles Kenyon** a Cambridge man from Bury was appointed captain. The team was strong in batting, weak in bowling but finished fifth in the championship. Two-day county matches were tried this season and many finished in a draw. War damage had to be repaired and membership went up to one pound six shillings with ladies paying ten shillings.

● *The previous year, women over 30 years of age were given the right to vote in parliamentary elections.*

Below: The team in 1919
Back (l to r): Jimmy Heap, Jim Tyldesley, Bill Brown, Dick Tyldesley, Ernest Tyldesley, Harry Dean, Charlie Harrows.
Middle: J. T. Tyldesley, George Shelmerdine, Myles Kenyon, Alan Boddington, Vic Norbury.
Front: Harry Rylance (Sec), Harry Makepeace.

AFTER the Great War ended in 1918 the process of rebuilding began. Stands had to be replaced and there was hardly any finance available. In 1919 county cricket began again and there were experienced batsmen available to Lancashire in Ernest Tyldesley, Harry Makepeace, Charlie Hallows, Jack Sharp and Frank Watson, Lol Cook, Cec Parkin and Dick Tyldesley. Ted McDonald was soon to join the County and other gifted cricketers followed, including Iddon, Sibbles, Duckworth and Hopwood. They were to make Lancashire the strongest side in the country over the next 10 years.

In 1919 membership was just over 2,000 with an annual subscription of two guineas. Crowds started to attend in their thousands, on one occasion as many as 36,000 on one day. Lancashire cricket was entering one of its most successful phases in the Twenties.

Lancashire in 1920

Back (l to r): Rylance (Sec), L. Cook, C. Hallows, R. Tyldesley, E. Tyldesley, Cec Parkin, J. Tyldesley, J.S. Heap.   Front: H. Makepeace, Reg Spooner, Jack Sharp, F.W. Musson, H. Dean.

In 1920 the crowds came back and well over 30,000 saw the traditional Bank Holiday Monday match against Yorkshire. Lancashire gained more championship points than any other county but finished runners-up to Middlesex on the percentage results method. Lol Cook took 150 wickets, Dean 124 and the skilful Cec Parkin was successful when he could play. Harry Makepeace, Ernest Tyldesley and Charlie Hallows batted superbly as did Jack Sharp who occasionally stood in for the absent Myles Kenyon.

Top: Test selector **Henry Foster**, **Archie MacLaren** and **Reggie Spooner**, watch the Test match at Old Trafford in July 1921.

Centre: **Charlie Hallows**, **Ernest Tyldesley** and **Cec Parkin**, all chosen to play in the 1921 Test at Old Trafford, watch the rain from their dressing room window on the first day.

Bottom: The crowd standing on the popular side of the ground at the 1921 Old Trafford Test match.

Above: **Jack Barnes** and **Charlie Hallows** batting for Lancashire against the 1921 Australians. Gregory is the bowler from the Stretford end. The tourists were guaranteed a large bonus if they remained unbeaten in all first class games. They achieved that record until MacLaren showed his qualities of leadership and put a team together to beat them. MacLaren was in his 50th year.

Left: In 1921 **Jimmy Heap** had his benefit and received £1,800 in his last season. The Burnley left-hand bowler had a rhythmic, easy style, taking over 400 wickets for Lancashire.

Below: An aerial view of Old Trafford in 1921. The route to the ground was by Warwick Road. Fields surrounded the ground where Talbot Road is now built.

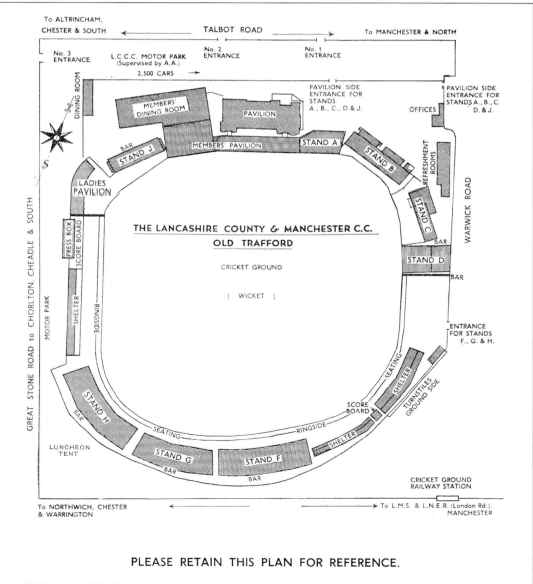

THE LANCASHIRE COUNTY & MANCHESTER C.C.

OLD TRAFFORD

CRICKET GROUND

| WICKET |

PLEASE RETAIN THIS PLAN FOR REFERENCE.

Above: A view of Old Trafford in 1922. It is the Roses game on the summer Bank Holiday weekend. In the final hour the result could have gone either way but finished as an exciting draw, with Lancashire needing just one wicket and Yorkshire requiring only a few runs.

The size of the playing enclosure was estimated at $5\frac{1}{2}$ acres.

● *This year the British Broadcasting Company was formed.*

Left: Plan of Old Trafford ground in 1923.

Lancashire in 1923

Back (l to r): George Duckworth, Walker Ellis, Frank Watson, William Hickmott, Dick Tyldesley, Ernest Tyldesley, Cec Parkin. *Front:* Lol Cook, Jack Barnes, Jack Sharp, Len Green, Harry Makepeace.

Above: Father **A.N.** with son **A.H. Hornby** who left Lancashire to buy a farm in Ireland.

Jack Sharp turned amateur to captain the side in 1923. George Duckworth who was to become England's wicket keeper made his debut. Behind the Pavilion a motor park was being created as the car became a popular mode of transport.

Left: **Jack Sharp** the new captain.

Below: Four Lancastrian-born players who played in 1923. *Left to right* - **Jack Barnes** a stylish amateur batsman who was captain occasionally when his Liverpool business allowed. He served in both world wars.
Alfred Hall a left arm medium fast bowler went on to play seven Test matches for South Africa.
Stan Ellis an off-break bowler whose father and brother also played for the County.
Edward Leach a steady batsman who later went to Somerset.

Above: Three distinguished captains, A.N. Hornby, Myles Kenyon and Archie MacLaren in 1923.

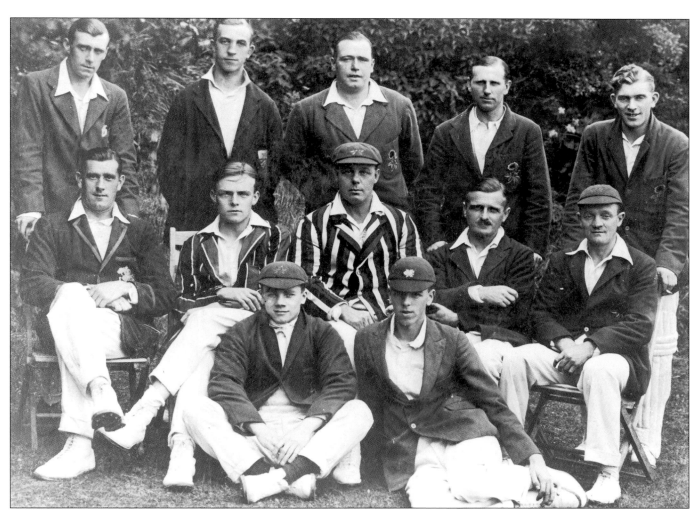

1924 was Lancashire's Diamond Jubilee year. The most exciting game was at Headingley where Yorkshire needed only 57 runs in their second innings to win. **Dick Tyldesley** and **Cec Parkin** bowled them out for 33.

Above: 1924 Team
Back (l to r): Charlie Hallows, J. Iddon, Dick Tyldesley, Ernest Tyldesley, Frank Watson.
Front: Cec Parkin, Peter Eckersley, Jack Sharp, A.W. Pewtress, Harry Makepeace.
On ground: George Duckworth and Len Hopwood.

Right: **Cec Parkin** was the most versatile of bowlers, turning the ball both ways with variation of flight. He took over 1,000 first class wickets including 200 in 1923 and 1924. Parkin played in 10 Test matches. League cricket attracted him where he could play for fun and receive a good living wage, so his first class appearances were limited.

The South Africans tourists played their 4th Test at Old Trafford in 1924. Less than three hours play was possible on the first day because of rain. The pitch was waterlogged the following day.

Right: A patient spectator sits in a temporary stand waiting for play to re-start ..... it didn't.

The England team at Old Trafford included George Duckworth on his debut. Jack MacBryan of Somerset played his sole Test match. He is the only Test player who did not bat, bowl or dismiss anyone on the field.

Below: England team *(left to right)* - Kilner, Duckworth, R. Tyldesley, Geary, Hendren, Sandham, Woolley, Douglas, Tate, MacBryan, Sutcliffe.

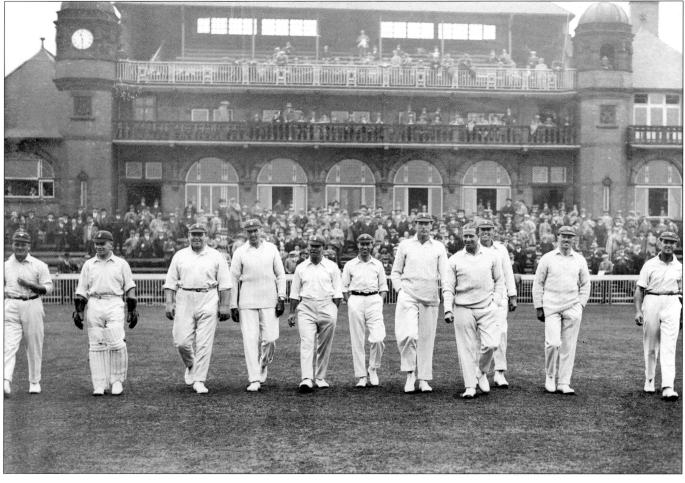

Left: **Don Davies** made his debut as an amateur batsman. He later became a Lancashire Committee member and Vice President. As an all-round sportsman he played soccer for Bolton Wanderers, won an England amateur cap and became a successful journalist with the *Manchester Guardian*. He was killed in the fateful Manchester United air crash at Munich in 1958.

Above: At the beginning of the 1925 season, **Jack Sharp** in his last year at Old Trafford welcomes spinner **Cec Park**. Behind him is fast bowler **Ted McDonald**. In that season the two bowlers took over 300 wickets between them.

Right: **Alf Pewtress**, an amateur from Rawtenstall, was vice-captain in 1925.

Right: On retirement, many Lancashire cricketers extended their career by taking on a business under their name. Those running sports shops included Alex Watson, Dick Barlow, Frank Sugg, J.T. Tyldesley and double international Jack Sharp.

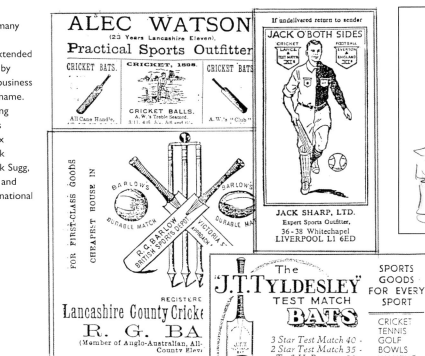

Above: An unpublished caricature of Len Green by the Australian cricketer Arthur Mailey.

Below: Having won the Military Cross in the first world war, **Major Len Green** (seen here batting in the nets), was a keen cricketer with Whalley when asked to captain Lancashire. He was an all-round sportsman playing rugby union and hockey at county level. In 1951-52 he became President of the club.

Above: Lancashire taking the field at the beginning of the 1926 season led by Major Leonard Green. The team went on to win the championship.

Above: Lancashire's success was partly due to **Ted McDonald** who took 163 wickets. He was a natural athletic bowler with smooth rhythm and exceptional pace. Having partnered Gregory in Australia's opening attack, McDonald came to Nelson to play league cricket before joining Lancashire. He lived in the county until his death in a road accident at 46 years of age.

Lancashire in 1926. *Back (l to r):* J. Iddon, E. Tyldesley, H. Makepeace, C. Hallows, F. Watson. *Middle:* Nash (Umpire), W.E. Howard, R. Tyldesley, E. McDonald, F. Sibbles, A. Woolley, Moore (Scorer) Buswell (Umpire). *Seated:* Rylance (Sec), O.P. Lancashire, L. Green (Captain), Sir E.F. Stockton (President), P. Eckersley, T. Higson. *Front:* G. Duckworth, M. Taylor.

Above: A group photograph taken in front of the Pavilion at Old Trafford in 1926. *Left to right:* Cec Parkin, Charlie Hallows, George Duckworth, Dick Tyldesley, J. T. Tyldesley (coach), Frank Watson, Major Len Green, Ted McDonald, Harry Makepeace and Ernest Tyldesley.

THE MANCHESTER GUARDIAN, WEDNESDAY, SEPTEMBER 1, 1926.

LANCASHIRE WINS THE CHAMPIONSHIP.

Right:
Lancashire win the
Championship at
Old Trafford, the
crowd run onto the
field in celebration
as Ernest Tyldesley
and Harry
Makepeace hit the
winning runs against
Nottinghamshire.

Championship Celebration
Dinner Menu 1926.

1926   THE CHAMPIONSHIP WINNERS   1926

J. Iddon   E. Tyldesley   H. Makepeace   C. Hallows   F. Watson
W. E. Howard   R. Tyldesley   E. A. Macdonald   F. M. Sibbles   A. Woolley   E. Moore (*Scorer*)
A. Nash (*Umpire*)   Mr. L. Green (*Capt.*)   Sir Edwin Stockton (*Pres.*)   W. Buswell (*Umpire*)
H. Rylance   Mr. O. P. Lancashire   Mr. P. T. Eckersley   Mr. T. A. Higson
(*Secretary*)   (*Chairman*)   G. Duckworth   M. L. Taylor   (*Hon. Treasurer*)

LANCASHIRE COUNTY
AND MANCHESTER CRICKET
CLUB

County
Championship
Celebration
Dinner

MIDLAND HOTEL   NOVEMBER 8th 1926
Manchester   *Monday*

Jack Hobbs and **Ernest Tyldesley** go out to bat against the Australians in the 4th Test at Old Trafford in 1926. Ernest was England's top scorer with 81.

Left: **Harry Makepeace** scored over 2,000 runs in 1926 as a sound, determined opening batsman. A popular all-round sportsman he played 487 matches for Lancashire between 1906-30 and represented his county in four Test matches against Australia scoring a century at Melbourne in 1920-21. A fine soccer half-back, he played for Everton in the F.A. Cup finals of 1906 (won 1-0 v Newcastle United) and 1907 (lost 1-2 to Sheffield Wednesday). As a senior player in 1926 he signed the photo "To the Skipper from Grandpa". When he retired he became Lancashire's coach for 20 years finishing his career at 70 years of age.

Below: Ted McDonald's heavy leather cricket bag.

Above: Lancashire, Champion County again in 1927.
Standing (l to r): E. Paynter, G. Duckworth, J. Iddon,
F. Webster, M. Taylor. *Seated:* C. Hallows, P. Eckersley,
Major L. Green (Captain), E. Tyldesley, F. Watson, R. Tyldesley.

CRICKET'S

LANCASHIRE AGAIN THE CHAMPIONS.

Sensational Notts Collapse Against Glamorgan.

SKITTLED OUT FOR 61.

Only Victory of Season for Welsh County.

In the most astounding finish to a
cricket season for very many years, Glamorgan

Right: **Dick Tyldesley** weighed about 16 stones, a cheerful
personality with a broad Lancashire accent. He was the
youngest and most successful of the Westhoughton
brothers (the others being William, James and Harry). His
leg breaks, mixed with a top spinner and occasional off
break, brought him 100 wickets in each of 10 seasons from
1922-31. He played seven Tests for England from 1924-30.

Right: **Watson** and **Hallows** opening the innings at Lord's in 1927. Frank Watson was a solid and dependable opening bat, scoring 1,000 runs in 12 seasons out of 13. He made an unbeaten 300 at Old Trafford against Surrey in 1928. He was an occasional medium pace bowler who took a useful 400 wickets for his county.

Frank Watson

Below: **Charlie Hallows**, a tall and stylish left-hander scored over 20,000 runs for his county. In 1928 he joined the distinguished company of W.G. Grace and Wally Hammond, the only three players to score 1,000 runs in May. Hallows deserved to gain more than his two caps for England but he was competing with Jack Hobbs. He finished his career as a coach at Old Trafford more than 50 years after he made his debut. He is batting here at Lord's in 1927 with Price of Middlesex, the wicket keeper.

Above: Lancashire's batting at Lord's against Middlesex in 1927. **Frank Watson** who scored a century is batting with **Charlie Hallows**.

Below: Captain **Leonard Green** and **Charlie Hallows** are applauded by the Lancashire members after beating Yorkshire by 8 wickets at Old Trafford in 1927.

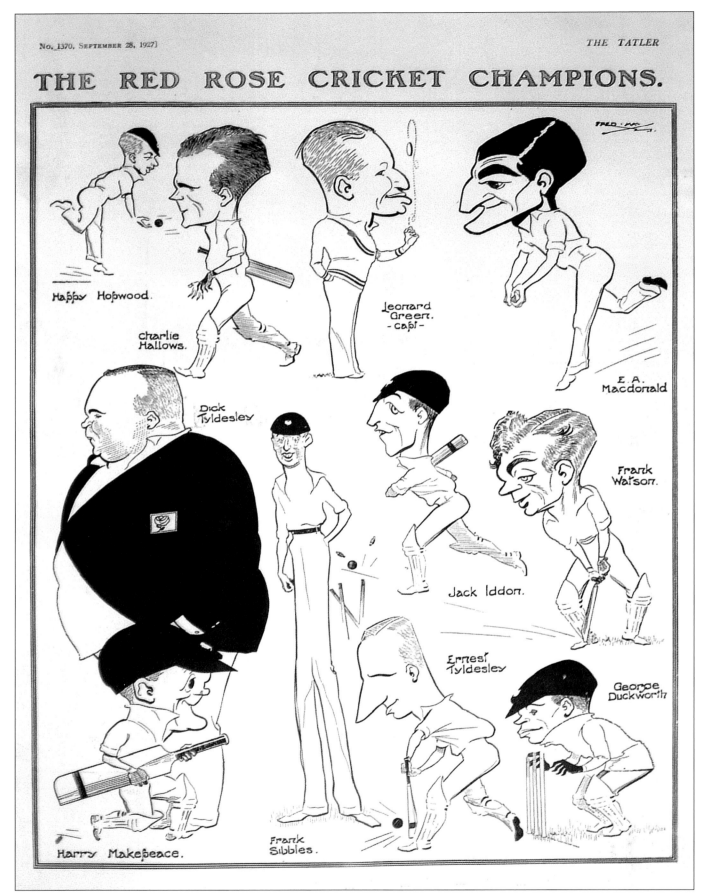

Fred May caricatures of the 1927 team.

Above: Major **Len Green** relaxing playing bowls. **Charlie Hallows** and **Ted McDonald** seated, watch for the turn.

Right: No indoor nets in 1928. The members' dining room was used for indoor practice!

Two officials pass a humorous comment and best wishes for the coming 1928 season to Lancashire players in the nets. From left to right H. Rylance Secretary, Sibbles, Iddon, Duckworth, Eckersley, Watson and R. Tyldesley, Dr Hitchon and Sir Edwin Stockton.

Above: At the beginning of the 1928 season Captain **Len Green** pads up for net practice with fast bowler **Gordon Hodgson**. The bowler also played soccer for Liverpool scoring 232 goals, a record until broken by Roger Hunt. He played football for England in three internationals.

Above: **Ernest Tyldesley** scored over 3,000 runs in the 1928 season, also making the first-ever Test century against the West Indies the same year. He was a slightly built but stylish batsman, an excellent driver and hooker of the ball playing in more games and scoring more runs for Lancashire than any other player.

Right: In 1928 **George Duckworth** made a record 97 dismissals for the county. An agile, stocky 'keeper with the loudest appeal in cricket, he made a record 922 dismissals for Lancashire in 424 matches and represented his country in 24 Tests. After his retirement he became a farmer, sports journalist and broadcaster, hotelier, baggage master to England touring teams and managed three Commonwealth teams to India. He was a Director of Warrington Rugby League Club.

OF THE RED ROSE: THE CHAMPION CRICKET COUNTY.

Caricature of the 1928 championship team.

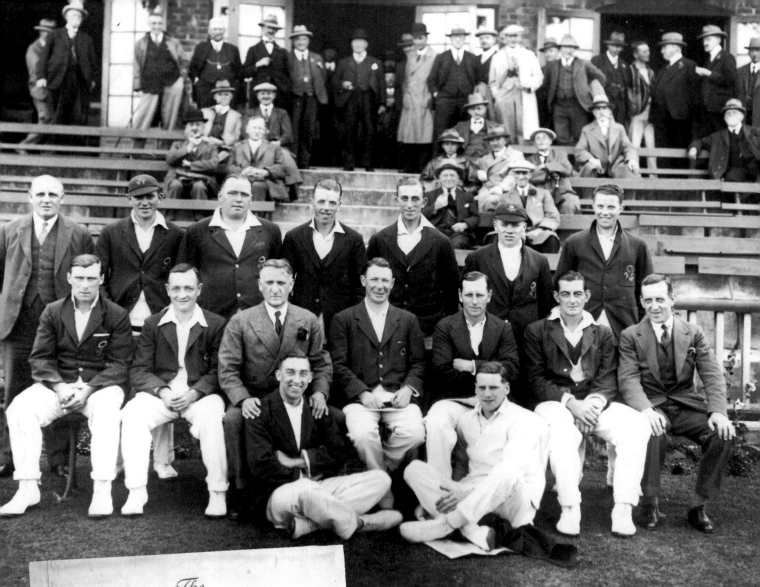

The
LANCASHIRE
COUNTY AND
MANCHESTER
CRICKET CLUB

COUNTY CHAMPIONSHIP
1926 1927 1928

DINNER

To Celebrate the winning of
THE
COUNTY CHAMPIONSHIP
for the
Third successive Year
1928

MIDLAND HOTEL
OCTOBER 16th 1928

LANCASHIRE CRICKET CHAMPIONS.

Third Successive Year.

NORTH SUPREME.

Title That South Has Lost Since 1921.

Many people think 1928 was Lancashire's best side; undefeated all season, they won the championship for the third year. Charlie Hallows, Ernest Tyldesley and Frank Watson scored over 2,000 runs each, Ted McDonald took 178 wickets and with all-rounders Jack Iddon and Len Hopwood it proved to be a well-balanced team.

Above: 1928 Team
Back (l to r): E. Moore (scorer), F. Watson, R. Tyldesley, J.L. Hopwood, J. Iddon, G. Duckworth, F.M. Sibbles. *Seated:* C. Hallows, H. Makepeace, T.A. Higson (Hon. Treas.), Leonard Green (Captain), E. Tyldesley, E.A. McDonald, H. Rylance (Secretary).
On Ground: T.M. Halliday and W. Farrimond.

Left: **Charlie Hallows** was a most popular player. He is in the centre, pictured at his benefit game when he received £3,000. On his left are **Ernest Tyldesley** and **Frank Watson** and right are **Dick Tyldesley** and **Harry Makepeace**.

Below: The Second XI, pictured here v. Notts at St Helens Recs, were also unbeaten in 1928. Eddie Paynter and Malcolm Taylor scored consistently with Jack Holroyd and Frank Rushton taking wickets. *Back (l to r):* J.D. Tipping, G. Taylor (Scorer), S. Chadwick, L. Hopwood, F. Rushton, T.M. Halliday. *Front:* J. Holroyd, L.W. Houseman, Dr J.B. Holmes, J.T. Tyldesley, F.D. Beattie, E. Paynter, L. Horridge.

Above: Preparation on the Old Trafford ground at the beginning of the 1929 season saw 'The Cricketer' model of the E-Smith Renovator in action.

Below: The 'Old Master' - **J.T. Tyldesley** coaching at the Indoor Centre in 1929. **Harry Makepeace** and **Eddie Paynter** are behind the wicket.

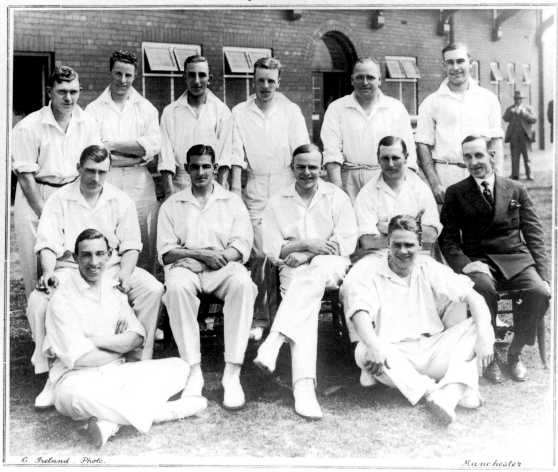

"THE SMILE OF SATISFACTION."

The LANCASHIRE COUNTY CRICKET TEAM.

WEARING THE **STORANCO** "SUPER" SPORTS SHIRT.

Patent No. 308145.
Reg. No. 739975.

C. Ireland . Photo.   Manchester

Messrs. STORANCO Ltd.,   OLD TRAFFORD,

    Manchester.   MANCHESTER,

                                                                JUNE 8th, 1929.

Dear Sirs,

                We, the undersigned, members of the Lancashire County Cricket Team,
have pleasure in informing you that we have given your Sports Shirt an exhaustive
trial, and we are all in agreement that it is truly a ═══

                "SUPER" SPORTS SHIRT.

Lancashire's success over this period as the country's leading side made them a popular team to use in advertising.
In 1929 they advertised Storanco sports shirts.

Above: View of covered stand and Ladies Pavilion from the members' area in 1929 at the Test Match.

Above right: The South Africans going out to field.

The South African tourists played the 4th Test match at Old Trafford in 1929 which England won, mainly due to the bowling of Tich Freeman who took 12 wickets in the match, George Duckworth assisting in six of these dismissals.

Below: Old Trafford Test: H.G. Deane, Captain of South Africa, stumped Duckworth bowled Freeman 0.

The regulations for Championship cricket were altered in 1929. The percentage win system was abolished and every county played 28 matches.

In 1929 the Club accounts showed a loss of £1,245. Almost half the matches were drawn partly because of the wet and cold season.

Left: Ted McDonald's benefit match against Middlesex in August was rain affected and he was awarded £1,947. Top wicket taker again for Lancashire in 1929, there is no doubt he was a major influence in the team's successful Twenties.

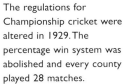

Above: **Dick Tyldesley,** a cheerful player on the field, took 154 first class wickets in 1929.

Left: **Peter Eckersley,** the newly appointed Captain in 1929.

Right: **Harry Makepeace** was made assistant coach in 1929. He was brought back into the side for 11 matches aged 48 yrs and topped the averages with 52 runs per innings.

NEWSPAPERS, PERIODICALS, ETC.
BY POST—THROUGH "SMITHS"

Annual Subscriptions.	Inland. £ s. d.	Abroad. £ s. d.
" Answers "	0 13 0	0 13 0
" Autocar "	1 6 0	1 15 6
" Bystander "	3 3 0	3 7 6
" Country Life "	3 5 0	4 0 0
" Cricketer "	0 17 6	0 17 6
" Daily Mail " (Overseas)	0 10 0	0 10 0
" Farmer "	0 14 0	0 15 0
" Graphic "	3 3 0	3 7 6
" Illustrated London News "	3 4 0	3 11 4
" Ill. Sporting and Dram."	3 1 0	3 8 10
" John Bull "	0 13 0	0 15 2
" Motor "	1 6 0	1 15 6
" Passing Show "	0 13 0	0 13 0
" Punch "	1 10 0	1 16 6
" Radio Times "	0 15 0	0 17 0
" Sketch "	3 3 3	3 12 4
" Sphere "	3 0 10	3 9 6
" Tatler "	3 3 0	3 11 9
" Times " (Weekly Edition)	1 2 0	1 5 0
" Tit-Bits " and Xmas Number	0 13 6	0 13 6

ASK FOR W.H.S. POSTAL PRESS GUIDE

W. H. SMITH & SON, LTD.
BLACKFRIARS STREET, MANCHESTER

The decade before the Second World War

Left: Peter Eckersley took over the captaincy in 1929 and continued until 1935 when he became an MP. Joining the Fleet Air Arm in 1939 he was one of the first cricketers to die in action in 1940, at 36 years of age.

ALTHOUGH the Championship was won twice in the Thirties many of the players in the successful Twenties had retired. Cec Parkin, Charlie Hallows, Ted McDonald and Dick Tyldesley were certainly missed and Ernest Tyldesley was over 40 years of age.

A new group was emerging, young players who made their mark before the Second World War cut their careers short. Eddie Paynter, Buddy Oldfield, Cyril Washbrook, Frank Watson and the experienced Ernest Tyldesley formed the backbone of the batting with dedicated bowling from Eddie Phillipson and Dick Pollard, Frank Booth and all-rounders Len Hopwood and Jack Iddon.

They were all grateful for a place in the team as unemployment reached three million, recovering only slowly through the Thirties. A published report found that half the nation was ill-fed, the north being amongst the worst areas.

There was an expansion of the road building programme, the Mersey Tunnel was opened and mass production brought down the price of cars. Driving tests were introduced in 1934 but most professional cricketers could not afford private cars and continued to travel long distances by public transport.

The ground being prepared in 1930. Britain was in the 'great depression', money markets crashed and millions were out of work.

104

Park your Car at the
County Cricket Ground Garage

LANCASHIRE

Season
1930

Season
1930

The

Lancashire County

and

Manchester Cricket Club

Applications for Membership of the
County Club should be made to the
Secretary, 26, Barton Arcade, Manchester

Subscription ... ...   Two Guineas
(and One Guinea Entrance Fee)

Juniors (under 16 years of age) One Guinea

Ladies ... ...   One Guinea

Season Tickets (Ground Side) One Guinea

Official Caterers—Agars, of Manchester.

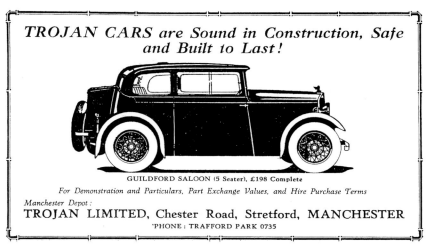

TROJAN CARS are Sound in Construction, Safe and Built to Last!

GUILDFORD SALOON (5 Seater), £198 Complete

For Demonstration and Particulars, Part Exchange Values, and Hire Purchase Terms
Manchester Depot:
TROJAN LIMITED, Chester Road, Stretford, MANCHESTER
'PHONE: TRAFFORD PARK 0735

Above: The new Guildford Saloon, £198 complete from a Stretford Garage.

Left: 1930 season fixture list. Members were encouraged to park their cars at the County Cricket Ground Garage (new car park).

Right: Bill Farrimond, who only played when George Duckworth was 'keeping for England, took seven victims in an innings against Kent to equal the world record. A quiet, efficient wicket keeper, he played most of his cricket in the Second XI but was good enough to represent his country in four Test matches.

Lancashire County Ground

LANCASHIRE v. KENT,

SATURDAY, MONDAY, TUESDAY, June 28, 30 and July 1, 1930.

KENT

#		FIRST INNINGS		SECOND INNINGS	
1	Hardinge	c Hallows b McDonald	16	c Hopwood b Tyld R	47
2	Ashdown	b McDonald	16	c Farrimond b McDon	6
3	Todd	b Hodgson	50	c Farrimond b McDon	33
4	Ames (wkt.-kpr.)	b Hodgson	31	c Farrimond b McDon	5
5	J A Deed	c Tyld R b McDonald	22	c Farrimond b McDon	28
6	T A Crawford	b Tyldesley R	1	c Farrimond b McDon	0
7	G B Legge (Capt.)	b Tyldesley R	0	c Farrimond b Tyld R	0
8	Fairservice	lbw b Tyldesley R	10	st Farrimond b Tyld R	0
9	Freeman	c Hodgson b McDonald	2	c Sibbles b McDonald	7
10	Wright	not out	34	c Sibbles b Tyldesley R	19
11	Peach	b McDonald	11	not out	1
		byes 1 lbs wds nbs	1	byes 1 lbs wds nbs	1
		Total	194	Total	147

FALL OF WICKETS.

FIRST INNINGS.										SECOND INNINGS.									
1	2	3	4	5	6	7	8	9	10	1	2	3	4	5	6	7	8	9	10
26	45	113	114	115	129	145	149	150	194	22	74	80	112	113	116	120	124	145	147

BOWLING ANALYSIS.

	FIRST INNINGS.						SECOND INNINGS.					
	Overs	Mdns.	Runs	Wkts.	Wds.	Nbs.	Overs	Mdns.	Runs	Wkts.	Wds.	Nbs.
McDonald	21.1	0	77	5	..	..	20	1	83	6	..	..
Sibbles	5	0	21	0	..	..	2	0	9	0	..	..
Tyldesley (R.)	19	6	61	3	..	..	9.4	1	25	4	..	..
Hodgson	7	0	21	2	..	..	10	1	29	0	..	..
Hopwood	4	1	13	0	..	..					..	..

LANCASHIRE.

#		FIRST INNINGS.		SECOND INNINGS.	
1	Hallows	lbw b Ashdown	2		
2	Watson	c Hardinge b Freeman	134		
3	Tyldesley, E	c Wright b Ashdown	117		
4	Hopwood	st Ames b Freeman	4		
5	Iddon	c Ames b Hardinge	10		
6	Sibbles	b Wright	7		
7	P T Eckersley (Capt.)	b Hardinge	5		
8	Tyldesley, R	b Freeman	22		
9	Farrimond (Wkt-kpr)	not out	46		
10	Hodgson	b Wright	7		
11	McDonald	b Freeman	28		
		5 byes 3 lbs wds nbs	8	byes lbs wds nbs	
		Total	390	Total	

FALL OF WICKETS.

FIRST INNINGS.										SECOND INNINGS.									
1	2	3	4	5	6	7	8	9	10	1	2	3	4	5	6	7	8	9	10
7	213	256	265	276	278	298	325	383	390										

BOWLING ANALYSIS.

	FIRST INNINGS.						SECOND INNINGS.					
	Overs	Mdns.	Runs	Wkts.	Wds.	Nbs.	Overs	Mdns.	Runs	Wkts.	Wds.	Nbs.
Wright	20	3	60	2	..	..					..	..
Ashdown	20	5	48	2	..	..					..	..
Freeman	55	9	129	4	..	..					..	..
Hardinge	22	4	70	2	..	..					..	..
Peach	18	1	51	0	..	..					..	..
Fairservice	5	1	24	0	..	..					..	..

Umpires: DENTON and BEET

Times of Play—1st day 11-30 to 6-30; 2nd day 11-30 to 6-30; 3rd day 11-30 to 6-0 or 6-30. *Lunch* 1-30. Tea Interval 4-15 each day

Lancashire were champions again in 1930, with Dick Tyldesley and Ted McDonald taking the majority of wickets helped by strong batting from Ernest Tyldesley, Frank Watson and Jack Iddon.

Back (l to r):
George Duckworth,
Frank Watson,
Len Hopwood,
Jack Iddon,
Frank Sibbles,
Malcolm Taylor,
Eddie Paynter.

Front: Charlie Hallows,
Ted McDonald,
Peter Eckersley (Captain),
Ernest Tyldesley,
Dick Tyldesley

The
LANCASHIRE
COUNTY AND
MANCHESTER
CRICKET CLUB

COUNTY CHAMPIONSHIP
1930

DINNER

To Celebrate the winning of
THE
COUNTY
CHAMPIONSHIP
1930

MIDLAND HOTEL
DECEMBER 15TH 1930
CHAIRMAN
SIR EDWIN STOCKTON
J·P

Above: Lancashire's fourth championship in five years was celebrated at the Midland Hotel in December 1930.

COUNTY CRICKET CHAMPIONS
1930
T.A. HIGSON

Above: The players were given an engraved cigarette lighter for winning the Championship. T.A. Higson was the Chairman of the club.

ORDER OF GOING IN.

1	Hallows
2	Watson
3	Tyldesley E
4	Iddon
5	Hopwood
6	P.T. Eckersley
7	Paynter
8	Sibbles
9	Duckworth
10	Tyldesley R
11	McDonald

Right: This batting list was pinned in the dressing room at Old Trafford for the first match of 1931.

Above: **Frank Watson** was granted a benefit in 1932. A sound opening batsman, he usually played the anchor role scoring over 20,000 runs for his County. The bicycle was a popular means of transport in 1932.

Left: **Malcolm Taylor** was a stylish left-hander who played 95 matches for Lancashire never really fulfilling his early promise. He was a cousin of Alan Wharton.

Below: April 1932, left to right: Charlie Hallows, Frank Watson, Bill Horrocks, Eddie Paynter, Ernest Tyldesley and George Duckworth are eager to have net practice.

Above: **Ed Barlow**, an Oxford triple Blue, played as an all-rounder in 1932.

Above: **Frank Sibbles** often opened the bowling with his medium pace swing but he could also bowl off spin when conditions suited him. In 1932 he took seven for 10 and 5-58 in the Roses match at Old Trafford.

Below: Lancashire played at Alexander Meadow, Blackburn for the first time in 1932.

Having had an excellent year batting for Lancashire, Eddie Paynter was chosen to tour Australia with Douglas Jardine in 1932-33. The Bodyline series angered the crowds and caused diplomatic interference. Unscathed came Eddie Paynter who had left hospital with tonsillitis to rescue England. He hit a six to win the Ashes. The ball presented to Eddie was auctioned after he died. It was bought for £4,400 by an Australian in 1990.

Top left: **Eddie Paynter** preparing for a net with **Cyril Washbrook.**

Top right: The ball with which Eddie hit the winning runs to win the Ashes in 1932-33.

Centre left: Webster's cartoon.

Bottom left: Eddie going out to bat with **Wally Hammond** whom he rated the best all-round cricketer.

Bottom right: Eddie Paynter.

What a Patient!   By TOM WEBSTER

TO-DAY'S NEWS ITEM

" PAYNTER, THE ENGLISH BATSMAN LEFT HOSPITAL — MADE SECOND TOP SCORE OF THE MATCH AND THEN WENT BACK TO HOSPITAL."

THE NURSE. "THERE ARE SEVEN AUSTRALIAN BOWLERS OUTSIDE MR PAYNTER AND THEY WANT TO KNOW IF YOU ARE GETTING ANY WORSE?"

Right: **Ernest Tyldesley** going out to bat with **Frank Watson** at Old Trafford against All India in 1932. Both scored big centuries with a partnership of 327 to win the game.

Below: The square is prepared early season in 1933. The Ladies' Pavilion, enclosure and open stand in the background was on the city side of the ground.

Lancashire's 1933 team contained six or seven all-rounders and would have been successful in one-day cricket. They lost only one championship match. *Front:* Frank Watson, Jack Iddon, Peter Eckersley, Ernest Tyldesley, George Duckworth. *Back (l to r):* Eddie Paynter, Cliff Hawkwood, Len Hopwood, Frank Booth, Albert Bennett, Frank Sibbles, Len Parkinson.

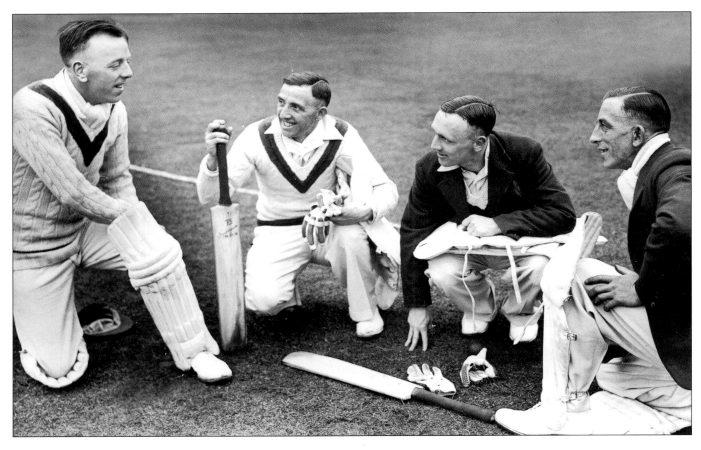

Above: **Len Hopwood**, **Eddie Paynter**, **Len Parkinson** and **Jack Iddon** pad up for net practice.

Below: **Len Parkinson** was a useful all-rounder playing 88 matches for Lancashire in the early Thirties. He was a leg break bowler taking nearly 200 wickets, leaving early in his career to play in the Lancashire Leagues.

● *In 1933 a new regulation came into force, stating that passengers for trams and buses must form a queue - waiting in line was unheard of before this year.*

Above: A welcome drink at Leyton in 1933. Left to right are Parkinson, Iddon, Sibbles and Booth. Len Parkinson took six first innings wickets against Essex.

Right: Jack Hobbs scored nearly 200 centuries, his last at Old Trafford playing in George Duckworth's benefit match. The members in the Pavilion sang 'Auld Lang Syne' as he came in.

Left: Ernest Tyldesley scored his 100th century at Peterborough against Northamptonshire. The team celebrated at The Bull Hotel where they signed the menu. The Lancashire club presented Ernest with a gold cigarette case for his 100 centuries.

Below: A signed menu from the celebration dinner at The Bull Hotel and the gold cigarette case presented to Ernest Tyldesley.

THE BULL HOTEL
PETERBOROUGH.

Menu.

LANCASHIRE C.C.
7 - 7 - 34
•••••••••
Cantaloup
••••
Consomme Glace
••••
Grilled Dover Sole Colbert
••••
Roast Duckling
••••
New Potatoes
••••
Green Peas
••••
Orange Salad
••••
Raspberry & Red Currant Tart
& Cream
••••
Cream Ice

Above: Champion County again in 1934; the team consisted of all Lancashire born players on many occasions.
Back (l to r): Cyril Washbrook, Len Hopwood, Jack Iddon, Frank Booth, Dick Pollard, Len Parkinson, Norman Oldfield.
Front: Eddie Paynter, Ernest Tyldesley, Peter Eckersley, Lionel Lister, George Duckworth.

Above left: A menu card for the Championship dinner.

Left: The Second XI were Minor Counties champions too in 1934.
Back (l to r): Greenhalgh, Pollard, Washbrook, Hawkwood, Phillipson, Wilson, J. Chadwick.
Front: Holroyd, H.R.W. Butterworth, P. Higson (Capt), H. Makepeace (Coach), Farrimond, Oldfield.

● In 1934 George V opened the Manchester Central Library, Stockport's Fred Perry was the Wimbledon tennis champion and in Manchester large marches were being organised by the fascist leader Oswald Mosley whose best man at his wedding was Adolf Hitler.

Above: A heat-wave came to Manchester for the 1934 Test match. England declared on 629 with Bill O'Reilly taking seven wickets. Australia with Bradman, McCabe and Ponsford narrowly missed following on. The four-day Test was drawn.

Left: Crowds sitting on the grass up to the boundary line at the Test match. England v Australia 1934.

Bottom left: Walters and Sutcliffe open the innings for England at Old Trafford.

Above: **Jack Iddon** was a handsome, elegant batsman of classical style and a steady left arm spinner. He is one of only four Lancashire players to have scored 10,000 runs and taken 500 wickets. In 1934 he scored 2,000 runs. In total he made 20,000 runs for Lancashire including a century against every other county. He played in five Test matches.

Right: **Len Hopwood** did the double in 1934 and again in 1935. He was a slow left arm bowler and right hand solid batsman. In 1934 he played two Test matches against Australia. The previous year he scored a century and took ten wickets in the match against Leicestershire at Old Trafford. In 1981 he was the first former professional player to become President of the club.

Above: Old Trafford was full when Lancashire played Yorkshire in Bank Holiday fixtures throughout the 1930s.

Above: Two private aeroplanes were chartered in 1935 by Peter Eckersley to take the team from Swansea to Southampton. They were the first County to travel by air to a match. *L to r:* Pilot, C. Washbrook, N. Oldfield, E. Phillipson, L. Parkinson, L. Hopwood, F. Sibbles, Pilot, L. Lister, P. Eckersley.

Below: Aerial view of the cricket ground in the early Thirties - the County Ground is bottom left, Manchester United F.C.'s Old Trafford ground top left and the greyhound racing track middle right.

M. S. J. & A. RAILWAY

ELECTRIC TRAIN SERVICE

to and from

Warwick Road Station
(OLD TRAFFORD)

STATION PLATFORMS ADJOIN
CRICKET GROUND

CHEAP RETURN FARES:

FROM	3rd Class	
London Road	5½d.	SPECIAL
Oxford Road	4½d.	SERVICE
Knott Mill	4½d.	OF
Altrincham and B. . .	9½d.	TRAINS
Navigation Rd., . . .	9½d.	every few
Timperley	7½d.	minutes
Brooklands	6½d.	on County
Sale	5½d.	Match
Dane Road	4½d.	Days
Stretford	3½d.	

Special Single Fares from Warwick Road
Station to

OXFORD ROAD   -   2½d.
LONDON ROAD   -   3½d.

FAST AND FREQUENT TRAINS

Above: Lancashire walking out to field in 1936. The Ladies' Pavilion is in the background.

Left: In the mid-Thirties, cheap return fares were available from the surrounding area to the Old Trafford Ground, then called Warwick Road Station.

Below: Lancashire played at the Westcliffe ground, Preston for the first time. Wally Hammond and Charlie Barnett scored centuries as did newly-appointed captain Lionel Lister.

Above: **Lionel Lister** took over the captaincy from Peter Eckersley in 1936. He played for Cambridge University, where he captained them at football, and represented England as an amateur soccer international.

Above: **Eddie Paynter** travelled all night to Hove after playing in a Test match at Old Trafford in 1937. Far from exhausted, he opened with Cyril Washbrook and posted a century before lunch in an opening partnership of 268. Paynter went on to score 322 in only five hours.

Left: 1937 aerial view of Old Trafford.

A NEW PRACTICE PITCH AT OLD TRAFFORD

A new concrete practice pitch being laid at the Old Trafford cricket grounds yesterday.

Above: Groundsmen lay a new concrete pitch on the practice ground in April.

Left: **Lionel Lister** leads his side out to play the 1938 Australians at Old Trafford.

Below: All rounder **Eddie Phillipson** took 5-93 in the first innings.

Above: Lancashire v Australia - rain again as the teams run from the field.

Below: After eight victories from ten matches Lancashire led the table before bad weather hampered further progress.
The 1938 Test match was abandoned without a ball being bowled.

Right: After the rain waitresses play on the practice ground.

Below: On the day of play at a Test match, turf was being re-laid - unique in Test match history.

Above: In 1938 **Len Wilkinson,** a 21-year-old leg spinner, took 151 wickets including a hat trick at Hove. He was chosen to play in three Test matches the following winter in South Africa.

Top left: **Sir Home Gordon** (left) and **Sir Aubrey Smith** watch from the Committee Room. Sir Aubrey was the only player to captain England on his sole Test appearance in 1889. Later he became a well-known film star in Hollywood.

Centre left: It was **Eddie Paynter's** season. Starting with a score of 291 at Southampton, he averaged over 60 for his County. In the Test match at Trent Bridge he scored an unbeaten 216 against the Australians.

Bottom left: **Eddie Paynter** with his four-year-old son and **Len Wilkinson** on their return from Tests in South Africa in March 1939. Eddie averaged over 80 in the five Tests.

Right: **Norman 'Buddy' Oldfield** was a delight to watch as a gifted stroke player. Eddie Paynter and he, neither above 5ft 3ins tall, put on 306 for the third wicket record in 1938 against Hampshire. The following year 'Buddy' was chosen for England and scored 80 batting with Len Hutton against the West Indies. War interrupted his promising career and later he went to Northamptonshire with Albert Nutter, returning to Lancashire as coach after he retired from playing.

Below: Lionel Lister was padded up ready to bat against Northamptonshire in August 1939 when he was called up to join his Territorial regiment. Iddon temporarily took over the captaincy. Lancashire's last game was at The Oval, but as the ground was being used to prepare for war the match was transferred to Old Trafford. The players had to travel from Dover and arrived at the Lancashire headquarters at 4am, some sleeping in the Pavilion before fielding. The third day was cancelled as the Royal Engineers moved in.

Back (l to r): Cec Parkin, Cyril Washbrook, Dick Pollard, Eddie Phillipson, Norman Oldfield, Albert Nutter, Jack Briggs. *Front:* Bill Farrimond, Jack Iddon, Lionel Lister (capt), Len Hopwood, Eddie Paynter.

In 1941 the Pavilion and stands were damaged. Old Trafford was used as a transit camp for troops and a storage area for the Ministry of Supply throughout the war.

War damage to the outbuilding at Old Trafford

Bomb damage to the playing area in 1941 viewed by Australian Prime Minister Robert Menzies. A sentry on the main gate was killed.

Rebuilding after the War

TOWARDS the end of the war rebuilding the ground and the team began. Friendly matches were arranged in 1944 and a victory 'Test' match the following year attracted crowds of 25,000 per day. An appeal was launched to help rebuild Old Trafford.

Available to play for Lancashire were some skilful batsmen: Washbrook, Place, Ikin, Grieves and Edrich, all rounders Phillipson and Wharton and the bowlers, Hilton, Tattersall and Statham made a balanced side. They shared the championship in 1950 with Surrey.

The period started with food rationing but gradually the standard of living rose for cricketers. Roger Bannister ran the first four-minute mile in 1954, land and water speed records were being broken. The school leaving age was raised to 15 years and there was a programme of University expansion. The first satellites were launched, ITV started broadcasting, the world of entertainment was widening, offering competition and more choice to sports fans following county cricket.

Below: The bomb damaged Warwick Road score box.

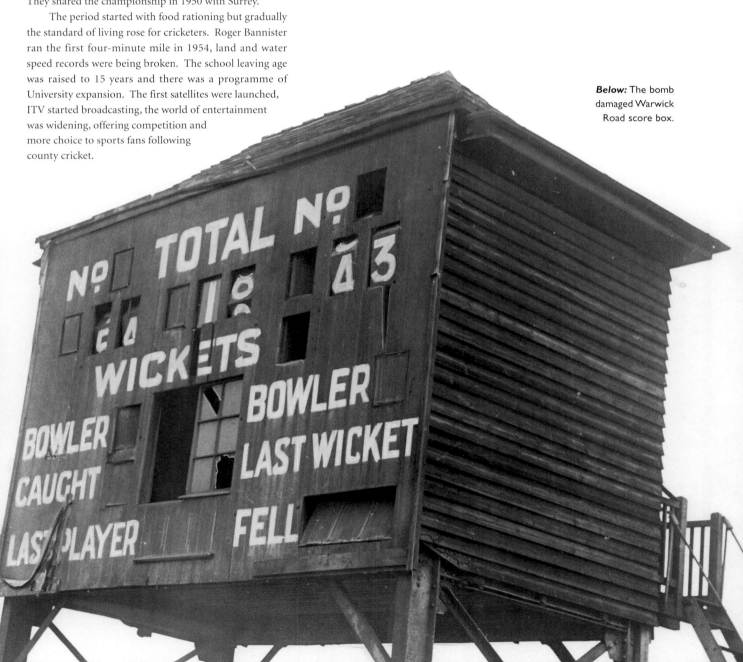

Above: In 1944 groundsman H. Williams prepares the ground for a charity game involving first class Ccricketers serving in the forces, the first match for five years. The army trucks can be seen on the right

Left: The German prisoners of war were paid three farthings an hour. (In today's money under 3p for an eight-hour day!)

Right: In 1945 a tablet was unveiled at the Westhoughton Cricket Club to commemorate the four Tyldesley brothers who played for Lancashire and the Bolton League club.
They were: **Harry**, right arm spin bowler who died aged 43 years; **James**, all-rounder died aged 33 years; **Richard**, leg break bowler died aged 46 years and **William**, left hand bat, killed in action in 1918 aged 30 years. The Westhoughton Tyldesleys were not related to the Worsley Tyldesleys, J.T and Ernest.

Left: England won the Victory 'Test' match at Old Trafford in 1945. **Dick Pollard, Eddie Phillipson** and **Cyril Washbrook** were representatives from Lancashire.

Below: The schoolboys came to watch England play at Old Trafford.

Above: **Dick Pollard** took over 1,000 wickets for Lancashire as an opening bowler. He was known as the 'Owd Chain Horse' for his willingness to bowl all day. On his Test debut he took 5-24 at Old Trafford against the Indians.

Right: Popular Pollard at the piano with L to R: Jack Ikin, Major Howard, Len Hutton, Jim Langridge, Peter Smith and Bill Voce on their way to Australia 1946.

Left: All rounder **Eddie Phillipson** had approached the 'double' in two seasons before the war. He was a successful middle order batsman and right arm fast-medium opening bowler, taking 100 wickets in 1937 and 1939. He later became a respected umpire standing in 12 Tests.

Below: After the war **Buddy Oldfield** and **Albert Nutter** went into League cricket and part-time jobs outside cricket because the wages in County cricket were too low. In 1948 they both joined Northamptonshire.

Above: In 1946 Jack Fallows was appointed Captain for one year carrying on with the amateur tradition. Lancashire had the most successful openers in the country with Cyril Washbrook and Winston Place scoring nearly 5,000 runs between them.

Back (l to r): W. Roberts, E.J. Price, J. Bowes, E. Moore (Scorer), R.G. Garlick, A. Wharton, E.H. Edrich, B.P. King.
Front: J.T. Ikin, C. Washbrook, J.A. Fallows (Captain), W.E. Phillipson, W. Place.

Below: Lancashire fielders early season are, left to right: Eddie Phillipson, Eric Price, Phil King, Alan Wharton, Cyril Washbrook, Jack Fallows, Winston Place, Bill Roberts and Dick Pollard.

Left: An appeal was sent out to raise funds to build a new Pavilion.
An architect's picture of the plan was enclosed. Fortunately the fund did not reach half the £100,000 sought and the ground retained its old Pavilion, repaired of damage.

Centre: Old Trafford repairs in progress but play goes on in 1946.

Below: Groundsman Williams and his dog supervise the pitch preparation for the Second Test against India in 1946.

Above: The Nawab of Pataudi, leads his Indian side out for the second Test against England. Following the captain are Abdul Hafeez, Mushtaq Ali, D.D. Hindlekar and Sarwate. The England team included Lancastrians Washbrook, Ikin and Pollard who took 5-24 in the first innings.

Above: The two most successful bowlers in 1946 - **Eric Price** *(left)* and **Bill Roberts**, both slow left arm spinners.

Left: **Bill Roberts** took 100 wickets in 1946 but played only four years more before he died in 1951 aged 37 years. He was a slow left arm spinner who relied on line and length. Roberts played in three Victory 'Test' matches for England in 1945.

Left: Lancashire v Yorkshire at Old Trafford in 1946 on August Bank Holiday when over 37,000 attended.

Overleaf: Those who could not buy tickets for the Roses game climbed the walls on Warwick Road.

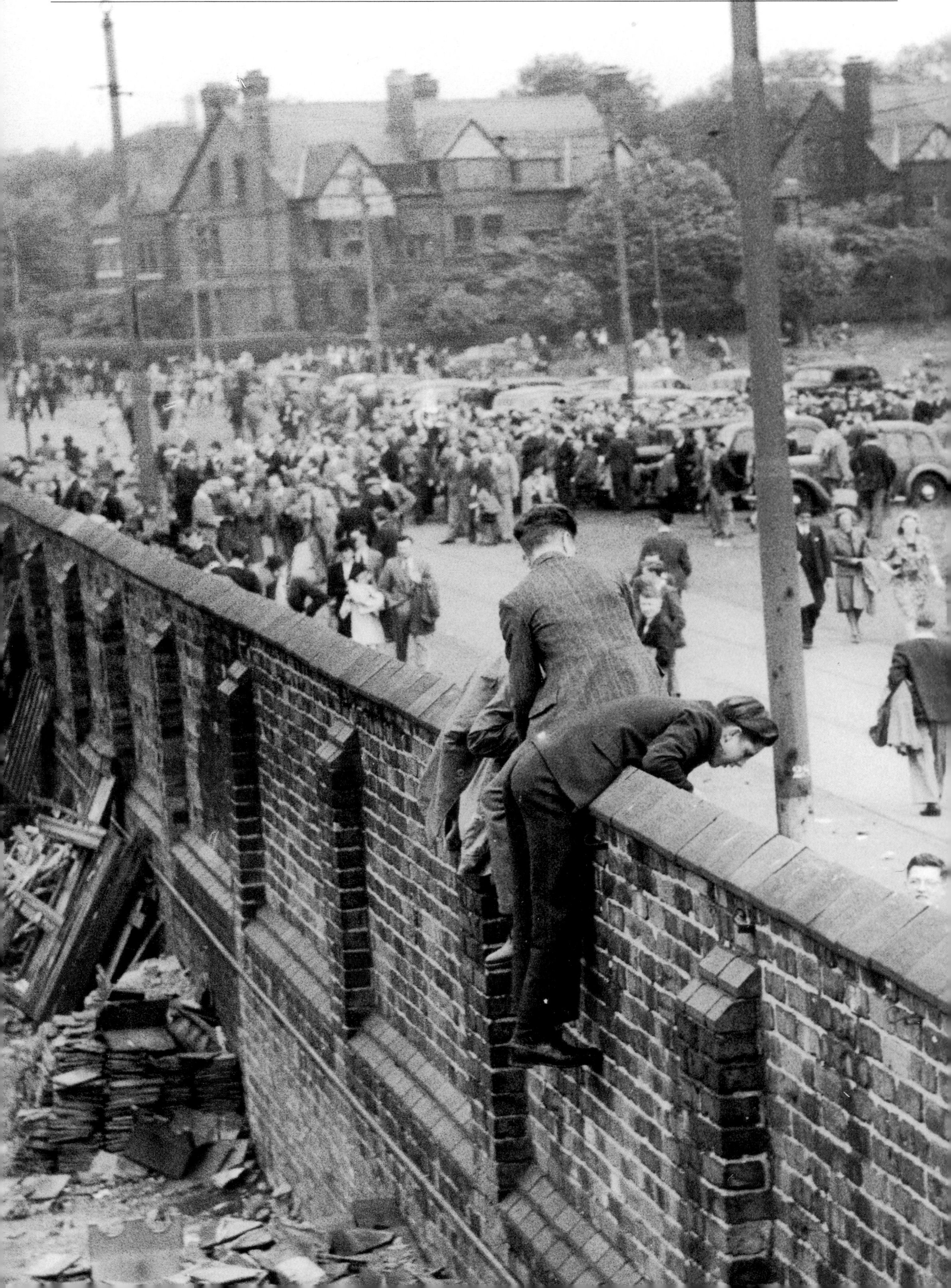

Left: Coach Harry Makepeace prepares the team for the 1947 season. From left (after the coach) is Eric Edrich, Jack Bowes, Cyril Washbrook, Alf Barlow, Alan Wharton, Eddie Phillipson, Nigel Howard, Bill Roberts and Dick Pollard.

Below left: The new captain, Ken Cranston, leads out his team for the first game in 1947 against Kent. Following the captain are Washbrook, Place, Phillipson, Ikin, Roberts, Garlick, G. Edrich, and Pollard.

Above: Alf Barlow made his debut as wicket keeper in 1947 playing over 70 matches for his County.

Right: Winston Place and **Cyril Washbrook** formed one of the most reliable opening partnerships in Lancashire's history. In 1947 they scored an unbroken first wicket partnership of 350 against Sussex at Old Trafford.

Below: Coach **Harry Makepeace** training boys at Old Trafford in 1948.

Left: Early season net practice with coach Harry Makepeace in 1948.
Left to right: Jack Kelly, Malcolm Hilton, Ralph Alderson, Roy Tattersall, Harry Makepeace, Ted Highton, Jim Hilton, Bob Berry, John Ingham and Tom Brierley.

Left: Rain delays the start of the Lancashire v Australia match in 1948. Spectators shelter against the white wall on the popular side.

Above: Don Bradman and Harry Makepeace inspect the pitch on a cool day in May 1948.

Above: Lancashire v Australia 1948. **Ken Cranston** has won the toss and invited Don Bradman's side to bat. Malcolm Hilton dismissed Bradman twice in this match.

Below: A thunderstorm ends the day's play at Old Trafford in 1948.

Top right: **Ken Cranston** captained the side in 1947 and 1948 playing first class cricket only two years. As a successful all-rounder he played eight Tests for England, captaining England once in the West Indies. Against South Africa he took four wickets in six balls at Headingley. Scoring over 3,000 runs and taking 178 wickets in these two years, he returned to his dental practice in Liverpool.

● *In 1948 the National Health Service began.*

Right: **Nigel Howard** took over as Captain in 1949. He was the son of Rupert who was Secretary 1932-48. Nigel played 170 matches for his County captaining them from 1949-53 and captained England in four Test matches in the 1951-52 Indian Tour. Washbrook, Wharton, Edrich, Place, Ikin and Grieves all scored over 1,000 runs in 1949.

Above: Lancashire 1st XI 1948. *Back (l to r):* E.H. Edrich, A. Wharton, J.T. Ikin, G.A. Edrich, M.J. Hilton. *Front:* W. Place, C. Washbrook, K. Cranston (Captain), R. Pollard, W.B. Roberts, T.L. Brierley.

Above: Lancashire 2nd XI won the Minor Counties championship in 1948. Bob Berry, Roy Tattersall, Nigel Howard and Malcolm Hilton went on to play Test cricket. Barry Howard, Nigel's brother, became President of the club in 1987.

Lancashire 1949

Back (l to r): Geoff Edrich, Alan Wharton, Alan Wilson, Ken Grieves, Malcolm Hilton, John Ikin, Winston Place.
Front: Bill Roberts, Cyril Washbrook, Nigel Howard (Capt), Dick Pollard, Barry Howard.

"*The War of the Roses*"

1849   1949

A Dinner
To mark the Centenary
of
YORKSHIRE – LANCASHIRE
County Cricket Matches

OCTOBER 7TH 1949   GRAND HOTEL   SHEFFIELD   YORKSHIRE

Above: In 1949 all-rounder **Jack Ikin** was top-scorer. He took a hat-trick at Taunton with his successful leg breaks and was a brilliant close fielder. He represented England in 18 Tests.

Left: A special dinner celebrated the Centenary of Roses matches in 1949. A century earlier the Lancashire and Yorkshire clubs were not officially formed but matches took place between the Sheffield and Manchester clubs.

Far right: **Tommy Higson** played a few games for Lancashire as an amateur. He became a Test selector and served on the Committee for 49 years as Treasurer then Chairman. His two sons played for the County.

Right:
Tommy Higson Jnr played 20 matches for Lancashire as an amateur. He declined the captaincy in 1946 and was elected President in 1977-78.

Above: Going out to practice at the start of the 1950 season.
Left to right: Jack Ikin, Brian Statham, Roy Tattersall, Nigel Howard (in blazer), Alf Barlow, Bob Berry and Ken Grieves.

Left: The two Hilton brothers discuss technique. Malcolm, on the left, took over 1,000 wickets as a left arm spinner. He made his Test debut in 1950. Younger brother Jim, an off-break bowler, stayed two seasons with his County before moving on to Somerset.

Above: Lancashire shared the Championship with Surrey in 1950. They beat Sussex, in one day at Old Trafford, the sixth one-day finish in their history. Rain prevented them beating Warwickshire after Washbrook's unbeaten century and Tattersall's 7-29. Surrey played at The Oval and caught up. Six Lancashire batsmen scored 1,000 runs and Tattersall headed the national averages taking 193 wickets. Eight of this team played Test cricket.
Back (l to r): K. Grieves, R. Tattersall, A. Barlow, R. Berry, M. Hilton, B. Statham, T. Dickinson.
Front: J. Ikin, C. Washbrook, N. Howard, W. Place, G. Edrich.

Above: The players were given an inscribed silver cigarette case for their championship win.

Left: A telegram congratulating Malcolm Hilton on his Test call, from popular band leader Jack Hylton.

Above: Standing room only at the Warwick Road end to watch the West Indies start an historic series with the first Test match at Old Trafford in 1950.

Above: In 1950 **Roy Tattersall** was the most prolific wicket-taker in County cricket topping the national averages with 193 wickets at 13.5 runs each. He went on to take well over 1,000 wickets for his County and played in 16 Tests. Competition from the established Jim Laker stopped him from being chosen for many more.

Above: **Bob Berry** made his Test debut the same year. He is seen here going out to bowl against Sussex with **Frank Parr** *(left)*, a wicket keeper who played 48 matches for Lancashire.

Above: Oldham-born **Peter Marner** made his debut for Lancashire at Hove in August 1952. He is seen here going out to field for the first time in County cricket aged 16 years 5 months, still Lancashire's youngest first class player. Left to right Bob Berry, Peter Marner and Malcolm Hilton.

Above: At the end of the 1951 season, five of the Lancashire side were chosen to tour India under the captaincy of Nigel Howard. The other England players were Malcolm Hilton, Jack Ikin, Brian Statham and Roy Tattersall.

Left: In 1953 **Bob Berry** took all 10 wickets in an innings at Blackpool v Worcestershire. He was a slow left arm bowler and played in two Test matches in 1950 against the West Indies, taking nine wickets in his first Test. Moving on to Worcestershire and Derbyshire he became the first player to be capped by three Counties.

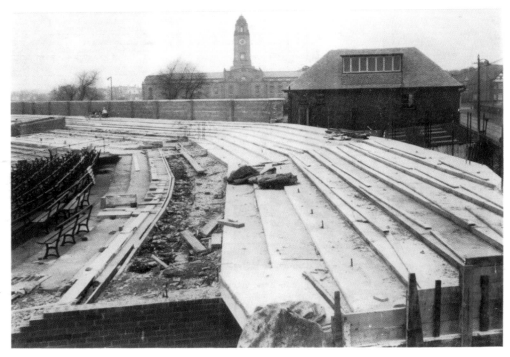

LEONARD FAIRCLOUGH NEWS

Monthly News Sheet of Leonard Fairclough Ltd., Builders and Civil Engineering Contractors

Vol. 3. No. 10   Adlington, Manchester and London   June, 1955

We still erect Stands at Old Trafford

Extensions to Stands B. and C.

Cricket fans at Old Trafford, Manchester, whether they turn up to see the County Matches, and especially the traditional battle royal between the Lancashire and Yorkshire teams — the battle of the Roses in Cricket—or to see the Test match between England versus South Africa, will see another new Stand extensions in front of the Score Boards and adjacent to the Pavilion, in front of the Secretary's Offices. This is the third instalment in the contract, which our firm has been engaged on for the Lancashire County and Manchester Cricket Club, since the termination of the war,

to reconstruct and extend the Stands in this world famous Cricket Ground. The new Stand immediately in front of the Score Board will be seen by all

_____

(Our Contracts No. 27)

_____

spectators on the other Stands, who will keep an eye on the Score Board.

The Fairclough Team on this contract, has had very adverse weather to com-

plete their task, as the accompanying photographs show. Despite all the snow, ice and frost, thhe job had to be completed on schedule in time for re-opening of the 1955 Summer Season, which will include the Test Match between England and South Africa, when we hope the players and spectators will enjoy warmer and sunnier weather than our Fairclough Team have had to endure. The contract has been under the supervision of Mr. Tom Davies, and later Mr. John Ind, with Richard Taylor as Foreman, aided by B. Tickle Ganger and E. Rylance and T. Heyes, Joiners. (See Photos page 4 and 5).

Left: In the first few months of 1955 major work took place at Old Trafford with stands A, B and C to the east of the Pavilion being rebuilt by Fairclough and Co.

Below left: Stand C goes up during the snows of February, certainly not cricket weather!

Right: The stand in front of the old scoreboard, next to the Members' Stand, was rebuilt.

Fairclough also built H stand, seen in the distance. Later a roof was placed over the stand. The whole stand was demolished in 1999.

Below: Stands A, B and C (later known as the Eddie Paynter stand) completely refurbished and being tidied after the Test match against South Africa in July 1955.

Above: **Winston Place** retired in 1955 having played nearly 300 games for his County. He had a good technique as an opener, scoring over 15,000 runs. Scoring a century in his last Test match in the West Indies, he should have played more than three times for England.

Above: Missing from the squad photograph (on page 158) is **Jack Dyson**.
When Lancashire beat Leicestershire by 10 wickets in 1956 at Old Trafford,
Dyson and Alan Wharton opened the batting. They were the only
Lancashire players to bat declaring unbeaten in both innings. This had never
happened before in first class cricket. Jack Dyson was an all-round
sportsman playing football for Manchester City. In 1956 he scored at
Wembley in the FA Cup Final when City beat Birmingham 3-1.

Above: **Alan Wharton**, a left hand opening batsman and right arm medium
fast bowler, played 392 matches for his County. He scored nearly 18,000
runs and took 255 wickets in his 15 seasons with Lancashire. He
represented England in one Test match in 1949 and played Rugby League for
Salford. After a three season spell with Leicestershire, he moved back to
his native Colne where he was a keen golfer.

Above: **Geoff Edrich** suffered as a Japanese prisoner of
war then went on to play 322 matches for Lancashire,
scoring over 15,000 runs. He was a successful captain
when required and an excellent slip fielder.

Left: **Ernest Tyldesley**, the first professional cricketer to
serve on the Committee, retired from the club having
served almost 50 years.

Above: **Cyril Washbrook** was recalled to the England side in 1956 to play the Australians in the 3rd Test at Headingley. England were 17 for 3 when he came in to bat but alongside Peter May who made 101, Washbroook scored 98 as the pair put on nearly 200 runs which helped set up an innings defeat of the tourists.

Right: Jim Laker took 19 wickets in the 4th Test against Australia at Old Trafford in 1956, a record unlikely to be broken. Ray Lindwall is the batsman.

Right: Earlier in the Old Trafford Test match a storm broke out and spectators rushed for cover against the driving rain.

Below: Jim Laker is presented with the two match balls following his momentous 9-37 and 10-53 in the comprehensive innings victory over Australia in the 4th Test.

The Lancashire squad in 1956. The team finished runners up to the strong Surrey side.

Back (l to r): P. Whiteley, A. Bolton, B. Booth, J.D. Bond, J. Jordan, E.A. Kelly, G. Clayton. *Middle:* J. Wood, W. Heys, A. Wilson, P. Barcroft, K. Bowling, T.S. Worthington (Coach), R. Collins, G. Pullar, S. Smith, F.W. Moore, D. Johnson. *Front:* M.J. Hilton, J.B. Statham, A. Wharton, C. Washbrook (Capt), G.A. Edrich, R. Tattersall, K.J. Grieves.

Above: Sixteen-year-old **Harry Pilling** arrives at Old Trafford in 1959. Coach Stan Worthington shows him around the Long Room in the Pavilion.

Right: **Harry Pilling** was one of the smallest players in County cricket. He was a very consistent number three batsman scoring over 15,000 runs. At 16 years, Harry is introduced to 6ft 2ins Roy Tattersall.

Above: **Charlie Hallows** coaching some keen youngsters in 1959.

Left: **Cyril Washbrook** retired in 1959. He was Lancashire's finest post war batsman and would have topped the highest aggregate had it not been for the war. A brilliant cover point, he played 500 matches for his County scoring over 34,000 runs and captained the side from 1954-59, the first professional to do so. With Len Hutton he holds the record opening stand in Tests for England, 359 against South Africa, averaging over 40 in his 37 Tests. He became President of the Club in 1989-90 and was awarded the C.B.E.

Below: Rochdale's **Tommy Greenhough** was picked for England in 1959 and took 5-35 against India at Lord's. He was a successful leg-break bowler who played over 240 matches for Lancashire. Tom kept fit exercising his dog on the hills near his home.

Above: Lancashire's first visit to Southport was made in 1959.

Below: **Brian Statham, Bob Barber** and **Geoff Pullar** are chosen for the first Test against the South Africans in 1960.

Above: In 1960 the team finished runners-up in the Championship with a new captain in Bob Barber. *Back (l to r):* J.D. Bond, K. Higgs, G. Pullar, R. Collins, P. Marner, B.J. Booth, K. Goodwin. *Front:* K. Grieves, A. Wharton, R.W. Barber, J.B. Statham, T. Greenhough.

Right: By 1960 a temporary press box was built over the Ladies' Stand and the club was the first to have a nylon cover to protect the whole cricket square.

Above: **Geoff Pullar** opened the England innings in 1961. As a stylish left-hander he played in 28 Tests between 1959-63, averaging over 40. He played 312 matches for Lancashire scoring over 21,000 runs in his career.

Left: Old Trafford from the air in 1961 when England were playing Australia. Almost 2,000 cars were parked around the ground.

Above: Three Lancashire amateurs. *Left to right:* **Major Rupert Howard** who scored an unbeaten 88 on his debut in 1922, became Secretary of Lancashire from 1932-48. He was father of Nigel and Barry and managed two MCC tours to Australia. **Major Leonard Green** played 152 matches and was elected President in 1951-52. **George Shelmerdine** played 31 matches, served on the Committee and became President in 1967.

● *In 1961 Yuri Gagarin became the first man to be launched into space.*

Roy Collins was a talented all-rounder, a hard-hitter and off-break bowler. He later became a popular League cricketer also playing for Cheshire.

Colin Hilton was a well built pacy bowler who played for Lancashire from 1957-63. Born in Atherton, he played for many years in the Lancashire Leagues around his home.

Above: **Bob Bennett** was second team captain in 1962 and went on to play 49 matches for his County. He was elected Chairman of the Club in 1987 - ten years before his election as Chairman of the England Management Committee on the English Cricket Board.

Left: **Gerry Houlton** and **Mike Beddow** enjoy a pint.

Below left: In 1962 wicket keeper **Alan Wilson** retired after playing 171 matches for his County over 15 years. A popular 'keeper, he was nick-named 'Ranji' for his low scores.

Below: Wicket keeper **Geoff Clayton** took 92 dismissals in 1962.

In many ways 1962 was the end of an era. The final payment was received from the War damage commission. The last of the Tyldesleys (Ernest) died and to commemorate the two great cricket families, the Tyldesley Suite was opened. The game of cricket was about to respond to the demands of the new generation.

Joe Blackledge, an amateur from Chorley, was appointed Captain for 1962 for one year.

Back (l to r): G.M. Taylor (Scorer), H. Pilling, G. Clayton, B. Booth, C. Hilton, R. Bennett, K. Higgs, J.D. Bond. *Front*: P. Marner, T. Greenhough, J.F. Blackledge (Capt), J.B. Statham, G. Pullar.

The Introduction of One Day Cricket

BY the early Sixties, county cricket was losing its audience and a fresh approach was required to appeal to spectators whose leisure hours were limited. Motorways were under construction and cars had become more affordable. Families were able to travel further and seek new forms of entertainment.

One-day cricket was introduced, sponsored by the Gillette company. Lancashire played the first ever game in April 1963 and almost immediately drew in the missing crowds. A further one-day competition, played on a Sunday, started in 1969 sponsored by Players Cigarettes. Fielding improved dramatically as Lancashire quickly found a successful formula for the shortened game. The players, enjoying the atmosphere and attention they received from the large crowds, gained amazing success. Overseas players were introduced, Clive Lloyd and Farokh Engineer brought a new cavalier atmosphere, particularly to the one-day game.

Partly for safety reasons as well as availability of play, all pitches were covered before play from 1981 which had an effect on bowling performances. The wearing of hard helmets became essential.

In 1963 Ken Grieves was appointed captain. He had a good season with the bat as did Peter Marner but Brian Statham needed more support with the bowling.

Above: Ken Grieves scored over 20,000 runs post war for Lancashire. He was a useful leg break bowler taking 240 first class wickets and a record 555 catches as a brilliant slip fielder. Ken Grieves was also a goalkeeper for Bolton Wanderers.

LANCASHIRE COUNTY CRICKET CLUB. 1963.
Left to Right. Back Row : E. M. Dalton (Physiotherapist). K. Goodwin. B. Booth. J. D. Bond. I. Leath. C. Hilton. K. Higgs.
J. Dyson. G. Houlton. R. Entwistle. J. Cumbes. K. Howard. R. Bennett.
Middle Row : P. Marner. J. B. Statham. K. Grieves (Capt.). T. Greenhough. G. Clayton. T. B. Reddick (Coach).
Front Row : J. Sullivan. K. Tebay. H. Pilling. R. E. Jones. P. Lever. M. Beddow. N. Wood.

Above: Lancashire won the first ever one-day match in the new Gillette Cup competition, a 65-over game. The preliminary round was against Leicestershire and **Peter Marner** won the first Gillette 'gold medal' as Man of the Match. The Kent and England Test player Frank Woolley presents him with the award at Old Trafford.

Below: In their centenary year, 1964, Lancashire played the MCC at Old Trafford. Three retired Lancastrians played for the MCC. In the first innings Washbrook at 49 years, Ikin 46 years opened with a stand of 139 and Roy Tattersall took six Lancashire wickets for 63.

Standing, left to right: T.W. Spencer (Umpire), K. Goodwin, P. Lever, J. Sullivan, R. Entwistle, G. Pullar, D.R. Worsley (all Lancashire), R. Tattersall, F.S. Trueman, R. Bowman, D. Murray, J.T. Ikin, D. Wilson (all M.C.C.), W.E. Phillipson (Umpire).
Seated: D.M. Green, K. Higgs, T. Greenhough, J.B. Statham (all Lancashire), K. Grieves (Capt., Lancashire), C. Washbrook (Capt., MCC), Sir Frank Worrell, D.C.S. Compton, D.B. Close, L. Livingston (all MCC).

Above: In 1964 **Sonny Ramadhin** signed for two years taking 92 wickets in his first year but losing form in his second.

In 1965 Brian Statham was appointed Captain and topped the Lancashire bowling again well supported by Ken Higgs. David Green scored over 2,000 runs without scoring a century.

Back (l to r): Bob Bennett, Peter Lever, Ken Shuttleworth, Ken Howard, Gerry Knox, Ken Snellgrove, John Sullivan, Bob Entwistle, David Lloyd, Mike Beddow, Ralph Alderson (Asst. Coach), Alan Thomas, Jim Cumbes, Keith Goodwin, Charlie Hallows (Coach). *Seated:* Sonny Ramadhin, Jack Bond, David Green, Brian Statham, Tommy Greenhough, Geoff Pullar, Ken Higgs. *Front:* Nigel Wood and Harry Pilling.

Left: In 1965 **Ken Higgs** opened the bowling with Brian Statham for England as well as Lancashire. He was an accurate fast medium paced bowler who successfully relied on movement from the pitch to take over 1,000 wickets before moving on to Leicestershire.

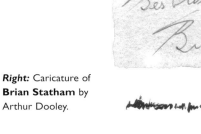

Right: Caricature of **Brian Statham** by Arthur Dooley.

Above: Geoff Pullar and Brian Statham welcome John Savage spinner, David Hughes all-rounder and opening batsman Graham Atkinson to the Lancashire squad in 1967.

Below: In 1967 groundsman Bert Flack was asked to prepare a pitch the other way round with the Pavilion behind the bowler's arm Batting proved difficult and the experiment was abandoned after this one game against the Pakistan tourists.

Above: Jack Bond took over the captaincy and led Lancashire, pictured here in 1968, to outstanding successes in one-day cricket.
Back (l to r): Taylor (Scorer), Wood, Savage, Hughes, Atkinson, Shuttleworth, Lever, Engineer. *Front:* Pilling, Statham, Bond, Pullar, Higgs.

Farokh Engineer was a brilliant wicket keeper making nearly 500 dismissals in his nine years with the County. He played 46 Tests for India.

Brian Statham retired in 1968. He was Lancashire's most successful bowler taking 2,260 first class wickets. A loose-limbed rhythmic fast bowler, he was consistently accurate, well over half his victims being bowled or LBW. He was also an excellent fielder. An example to all both on the field and off, he was awarded the CBE for services to cricket. He captained the side from 1965-7 and played in 70 Test matches taking 252 wickets. Brian Statham was elected President of the club in 1997-8.

Above: Watching the game from the Players' Balcony in 1968. Seated, **Brian Statham**, behind him **Ken Higgs** who took 100 wickets this season. **Peter Lever** and behind him **Farokh Engineer** in his first season at Lancashire.

Left: Statham's 250th Test victim, South Africa's 'Tiger' Lance, The Oval 1965.

Right: Last day's play at Old Trafford 1968.

Best wishes Cedric,
Brian Statham

Lancashire won the first Sunday League competition, The John Player Trophy In 1969 under Jack Bond's captaincy. The competition was broadcast on BBC each week.

Left: Jack Bond being presented with the Trophy.

Below: Back (l to r): Simmons, Sullivan, Snellgrove, Pilling, Bond, Lloyd (hidden), Jim Laker (Commentator), Bailey, Wood, Hayes, Durdon-Smith (Commentator), Hughes.
Front: Shuttleworth, Lever.

By kind permission of "PUNCH"

Above: A cartoon capturing Lancashire's Sunday League championship celebrations was featured on the front of the 1970 Year Book.

Right: A new indoor sports centre was opened in 1969 which gave the players three lanes to practice in when the weather was bad. Two squash courts were included.

Below: The West Indies tourists brought the crowds to Old Trafford in June 1969 with people spilling on to the grass.

● *This year the first man set foot on the moon in July and in England the voting age was reduced from 21 years to 18.*

LANCASHIRE 1970

Standing (L to R): G. M. Taylor (Scorer), B. Wood, M. Staziker, K. Snellgrove, F. Hayes, .P. Gooch, J. Simmons, D. Hughes,
D. Bailey J. Sullivan, C. H. Lloyd, K. Goodwin, G. Atkinson, N. Oldfield (Coach), D. V. Parker
Seated (L to R): D. Lloyd, K. Shuttleworth, H. Pilling, J. D. Bond (Captain), P. Lever, F. M. Engineer, J. Savage

Above: Jack Bond's side won the Gillette Cup Final at Lord's in September 1970. They also won the Sunday League John Player Trophy and came in the top three in the Championship table. In the Gillette Cup Final 1970 Harry Pilling was Man of the Match at Lord's when Lancashire beat Sussex.

Left: A postcard featuring the 1970 squad.

Two Lancashire opening fast bowlers made their Test debut against the Australians in 1970.
Above: **Ken Shuttleworth** *(left)* **Peter Lever** *(right).*

Two players who performed well in the successful Cup runs in the Seventies.
Left: **Ken Snellgrove** *Below:* **John Sullivan**

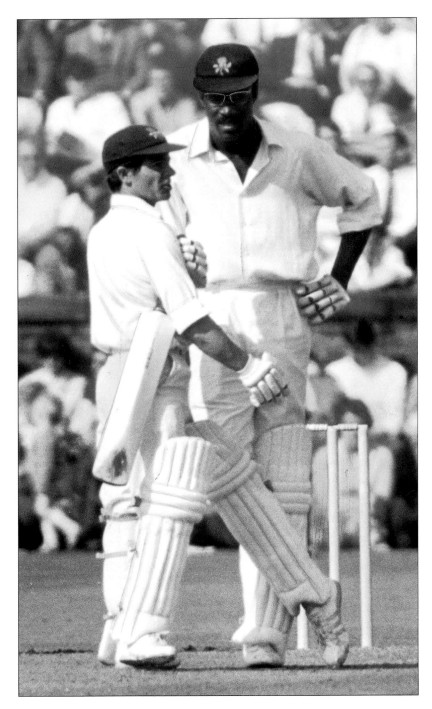

Above: A study in contrast - **Harry Pilling** and **Clive Lloyd** at the wicket in 1970.

Right: Catching practice at the beginning of 1971 season - Harry Pilling tests out the reflexes of Frank Hayes, Keith Goodwin (with gloves), Farokh Engineer and Ken Snellgrove.

Above: The crowd was so large for the 1971 Gillette Cup semi-final against Gloucestershire that many thousands were locked out of Old Trafford.

Left: Crowds inside spill on to the grass.

Left: Lancashire triumph at 8.55pm in the famous Gillette Cup semi-final against Gloucestershire on 28th July 1971.

Centre left: **David Hughes** celebrates with 24 glasses of champagne after his 24 runs in one over made him Man of the Match in the most dramatic of semi-final's.

Below: Lancashire walk out to field in the 1971 Gillette Cup Final at Lord's.

Above: **Farokh Engineer** congratulates **Jack Bond** who holds the trophy after Lancashire's 24 run victory over Kent in the 1971 final.

Right: They drank the rest - Jack Simmons joining in.

Left: Lancashire met Kent at Old Trafford in the semi-final of the Gillette Cup in August 1972, watched by a crowd of over 20,000.

Above: The treble - Jack Bond holds up the Gillette Cup in 1972.
Right: Cup Final programme - Lancashire win three in a row.

Below: In 1972 Lancashire won the Gillette Cup for the third year, beating Warwickshire at Lord's in September. *From left to right:* Chairman Cedric Rhoades, Farokh Engineer, Jack Simmons and Jack Bond. Clive Lloyd was Man of the Match for his magnificent century.

The Gillette Cup Final
LANCASHIRE v WARWICKSHIRE
at Lord's

GILLETTE CUP WINNERS

15p
Official Souvenir
Programme

SATURDAY 2nd SEPTEMBER 1972

Right: The whole team are in this picture in 1972 as umpire Bill Alley gives Yorkshire's Chris Clifford LBW, bowled Jack Simmons, to give Lancashire an innings win.

Below: Leapfrogging to the nets early 1973 season. At the back, Ken Shuttleworth over Ken Snellgrove, Peter Lever over Frank Hayes, David Lloyd over Farokh Engineer watched by Peter Lee.

Below right centre: **David Lloyd** was Lancashire's captain for five years from 1973. He played nine Test matches scoring an unbeaten 214 against India at Edgbaston in 1974. His versatile and quick witted personality enabled him to make a success of a variety of jobs after playing days. For the TCCB he marketed 'Kwik Cricket' in schools, became the Lancashire and England coach, was a popular radio and TV commentator and in demand as an after dinner speaker.

Far right: **Barry Wood** was a sound and combative opening batsman, an excellent fielder and useful medium pace bowler. Playing 260 first class matches for Lancashire he went on to represent his country in 12 Test matches. As an all-rounder he was very successful in one-day competitions for Lancashire and England.

Top left: Lancashire, the most successful team of their era in one-day competitions, won the Gillette Cup again in 1975, beating Middlesex by seven wickets at Lord's.
Left to right: Barry Wood, Frank Hayes, Peter Lever (hidden) Farokh Engineer, David Lloyd (with the cup), Clive Lloyd, Andrew Kennedy, Peter Lee and David Hughes.

Above: Lancashire regulars in the Seventies, from the left Bernard Reidy, Jack Simmons, Bob Radcliffe, Andrew Kennedy and David Lloyd.

Left: Peter Lee was a medium fast opening bowler with untiring energy. He became the leading wicket-taker in the Championship in 1973 and 1975 with over 100 wickets both seasons.

Right: Sir Neville Cardus died in 1975. He started writing about Lancashire cricket in 1919 under the title of 'The Cricketer' in the *Manchester Guardian*. The first writer to comment on the players' personalities and style of play, his descriptions in the many cricket books published under his name are regarded as classics of cricket prose. He was awarded a Knighthood in 1967 and became President of the club in 1971.

Far right: The bust of Neville Cardus by Nigel Boonham is exhibited at the Manchester Free Trade Hall.

In 1978 Frank Hayes took the captaincy for three years. The overseas players were Clive Lloyd and Colin Croft (missing from this photograph).

Back (l to r): John Lyons, Christopher Scott, Graeme Fowler, Ian Cockbain.

Middle: Geoffrey Trim, Bob Arrowsmith, Paul Robinson, Paul Allott, Andrew Kennedy, William Hogg, Bob Ratcliffe, Bernard Reidy, John Abrahams, John Savage (Coach).

Front: David Hughes, Barry Wood, David Lloyd, Frank Hayes (Captain), Jack Simmons, Harry Pilling, Peter Lee.

Above: Lancashire Cricketers who played in Tests against Australia fly out to celebrate the 1977 Centenary Test in Melbourne.
Back (l to r): Peter Lever, Ken Shuttleworth, David Lloyd, John Ikin, Geoff Pullar, Roy Tattersall, Cyril Washbrook, Bob Barber.
Front: Brian Statham, Audrey Statham, Eddie Paynter, Phyllis Ikin.

Left: **Frank Hayes** scored an unbeaten 106 on his Test debut in 1973. A gifted, hard-hitting batsman, he captained his County team from 1978-80.

Below: In 1980 Jack Bond returned as manager. A balaclava keeps him warm in early April.

Clive Lloyd was appointed captain in 1981 topping the batting averages again - Michael Holding played only seven matches for Lancashire taking 40 wickets.
Above: Back: John Abrahams, Chris Scott, Doug Beckett, Steve O'Shaughnessy, Neal Radford, Mark Wallwork, Roger Watson.
Middle: Jack Bond (Manager), Jack Simmons, Ian Cockbain, Paul Allott, Michael Holding, Bernard Reidy, Graeme Fowler, John Savage (Coach).
Front: David Hughes, Peter Lee, David Lloyd, Clive Lloyd (capt), Frank Hayes, Harry Pilling, Andrew Kennedy.

Below: Another cup - the Lambert & Butler Floodlit Trophy was won at Chelsea FC's Stamford Bridge ground in September 1981. Lancashire's winning eight-man squad celebrate *(l to r):* Doug Beckett, David Hughes, Paul Allott, Clive Lloyd, Andy Kennedy, Michael Holding, Graeme Fowler and Jack Simmons.

Above left:
Accrington-born, dashing left-hander **Graeme Fowler** scored a century with a runner in each innings v Warwickshire at Southport in 1982. He played 21 Test matches.

Above right: A medium fast accurate opening bowler, **Paul Allott** played over 200 games for Lancashire and represented England in 13 Test matches.

Left: View from the Hornby Stand where Stands A, B and C (now the Eddie Paynter stand) were constructed in the winter of 1982-83.

192

View from the Pavilion showing the stand under construction, it contained the new club shop, bar and museum.

In 1984 John Abrahams was appointed captain. In the absence of Clive Lloyd, captaining the West Indies, the club played left-handed all-rounder Steve Jeffries from South Africa, signed the previous season.

Above: Cricket Manager Jack Bond celebrates winning the 1984 Benson & Hedges Trophy with Steve O'Shaughnessy, Chris Maynard, Graeme Fowler, Paul Allott (hidden), Neil Fairbrother, Steve Jeffries (hidden), John Stanworth and Mike Watkinson. John Abrahams was awarded the Man of the Match against Warwickshire for his captaincy.

Above: John Abrahams holding the B & H Cup.

Right: Paul Allott shakes a bottle of bubbly shared by Steve O'Shaughnessy (left) John Abrahams (right with wine glasses) and Mike Watkinson, behind David Makinson.

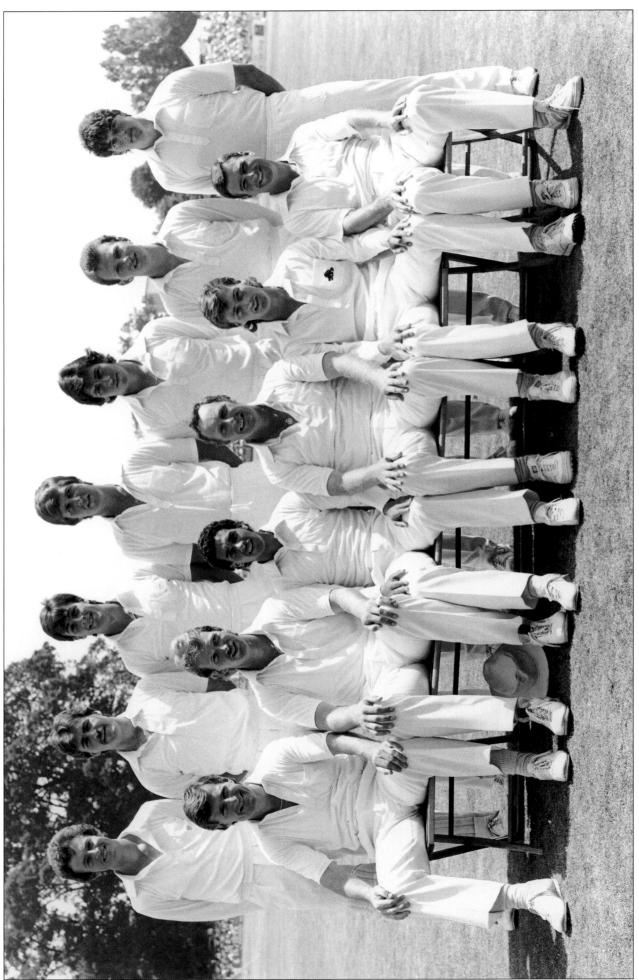

Lancashire 1984

Back (l to r): John Stanworth, Steve O'Shaughnessy, Mike Watkinson, David Makinson, Steve Jeffries, Neil Fairbrother, Ian Folley.
Front: David Hughes, Paul Allott, John Abrahams (capt), Jack Simmons, Graeme Fowler, Alan Ormrod.

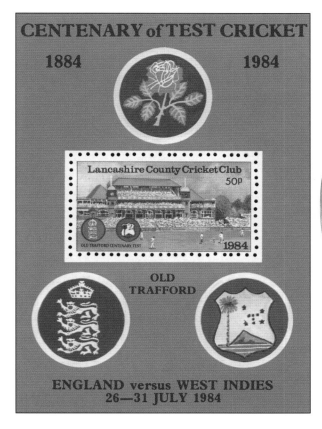

Above left and right: In 1984 Old Trafford celebrated its Centenary of staging Test cricket.

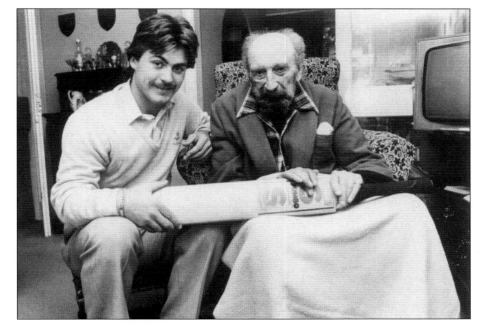

Left: Steve O'Shaughnessy scored 105 in 35 minutes at Old Trafford as the Leicestershire bowlers fed him for a declaration. It equalled Percy Fender's world record time for a century for Surrey against Northamptonshire in 1920. O'Shaughnessy met Fender at the former Surrey player's home at the end of the season.

Below: Lancashire played at Lytham for the first time in 1985, the twelfth ground to host a county game.

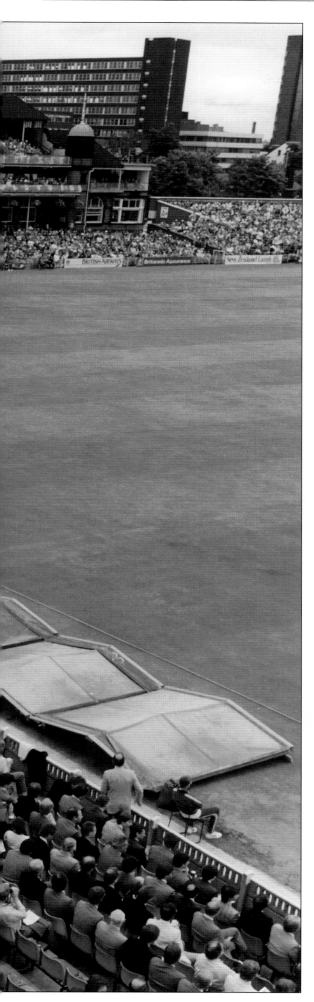

Left: View from the new executive boxes in 1985. The Australians were visitors for the Fourth Test at Old Trafford - England winning the Ashes series 3-1.

Above: **Clive Lloyd** was brought back as Captain in 1986. He was a powerful and entertaining batsman who captained Lancashire from 1981-83 and again in 1986. Bringing success to his chosen County, he helped them win many one-day competitions. Clive Lloyd captained the West Indies for a record 74 times playing 110 Tests and scoring over 7,500 runs for his country. He was an occasional swing bowler and in many people's opinion the best fielder ever seen.

Above: The council car park at the City end was used by members before the ground was purchased by Kellogg's.

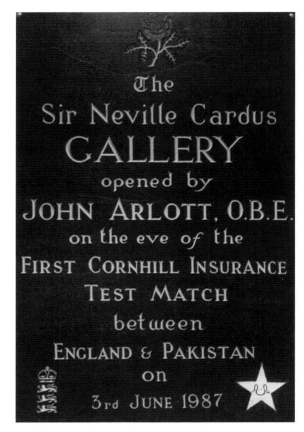

The
Sir Neville Cardus
GALLERY
opened by
JOHN ARLOTT, O.B.E.
on the eve of the
FIRST CORNHILL INSURANCE
TEST MATCH
between
ENGLAND & PAKISTAN
on
3rd JUNE 1987

In 1987 The Red Rose building was opened for members and gave the press the best facilities in the country.

Above: Two popular and accomplished all-rounders: David Hughes became a successful captain and Jack Simmons was elected Chairman of the Club in 1998.

Above: 1988 aerial view showing the Old Trafford cricket ground in the centre and the Manchester Ship Canal in the top of the picture. Manchester United's Old Trafford football ground is between the two.

Above: Lancashire became the first holders of the Refuge Assurance Cup in 1988 beating Worcestershire in the final at Edgbaston.
Back (l to r): Trevor Jesty, Andrew Hayhurst, Patrick Patterson, Phil DeFreitas, Dexter Fitton, Michael Atherton.
Front: Warren Hegg, Mike Watkinson, Paul Allott, David Hughes, Graeme Fowler, Neil Fairbrother, Gehan Mendis.

Above: In 1989 the team celebrate after winning the Sunday League competition sponsored by Refuge Assurance. From left to right are: Alan Ormond (Manager), Gehan Mendis, Wasim Akram, Paul Allott, Trevor Jesty, David Hughes (holding the trophy), Andy Hayhurst, Jack Simmons, Neil Fairbrother, Mike Watkinson, Phil DeFreitas, Warren Hegg and Ian Austin.

A good season in 1989, reaching the quarter finals in both the NatWest Trophy and the B&H Cup, 4th in the Championship table and winning the Sunday League competition sponsored by Refuge Assurance.

Back (l to r): Bill Davies (scorer), Ian Austin, Phil DeFreitas, Wasim Akram, Trevor Jesty, Warren Hegg, Alan Ormrod (Manager).

Front: Mike Watkinson, Graeme Fowler, Paul Allott, David Hughes (capt), Jack Simmons, Neil Fairbrother, Gehan Mendis.

In 1990 Lancashire won the first of their 'doubles', the Benson & Hedges Cup and the NatWest Trophy. This was the first time any County had achieved this. The team dressed up in 19th Century costume.

Back (l to r): Ian Austin, Neil Fairbrother, Graham Lloyd, Phil DeFreitas, Trevor Jesty, Mike Atherton, Mike Watkinson. *Middle*: Wasim Akram, Paul Allott, David Hughes (capt), Graeme Fowler. *Front*: Warren Hegg and Dexter Fitton.

Into the Millennium

IN the 1990's Lancashire's first XI continued their success by taking eight trophies, more than any other county. The second XI won the Bain Clarkson Trophy at the beginning of the decade and the Second XI Championship in 1997.

A Lord's final had become a regular occasion. There were eight or nine internationals in the side and with Test match calls, it was the one day games when all the players were available to play for Lancashire. The games drew the crowds in their thousands.

During this decade the ground saw some rapid development. First the club offices were extended, outwards and upwards. The double decker stand replaced the old Wilson Stand. New seating was installed around the ground. The Pavilion was extended providing a lift and new reception. The largest indoor school in the country was built in 1997. A 68 bedroom complex, the Trafford Lodge was opened at the end of the decade.

The club's turnover more than tripled in the 90's. It was a club looking to the Millennium, leading the other 17 counties in both business and success on the field.

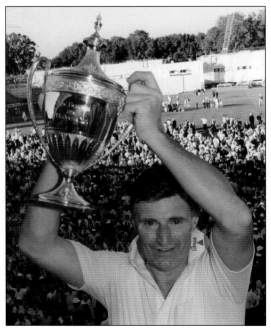

Above: Captain David Hughes lifts the NatWest Trophy in 1990...

Right: ...and the Benson & Hedges Cup at Lord's.

Left: The 1990 double winning squad enjoy a bit of fun with the photographers at Lancashire's annual pre-season photocall.

Back (l to r): Jason Gallian, Tim Orrell, Gary Yates, Marcus Sharp, Ronnie Irani, Nick Derbyshire, Nick Speak, Dexter Fitton, Graham Lloyd.
Middle: Lawrie Brown (Physio), Alan Ormrod (Manager), Ian Austin, Warren Hegg, Steve Titchard, Peter Martin, John Stanworth, Trevor Jesty, John Savage (2nd XI Coach), Bill Davies (Scorer).
Front: Gehan Mendis, Wasim Akram, Graeme Fowler, Paul Allott, David Hughes (Captain), Neil Fairbrother, Mike Atherton, Phil DeFreitas, Mike Watkinson.

Right: Phil DeFreitas took the Man of the Match award in the 1990 NatWest Trophy final against Northamptonshire with a devastating spell of 5 for 26.

Below: Man of the Match in the 1990 Benson & Hedges Cup final Mike Watkinson with Wasim Akram.

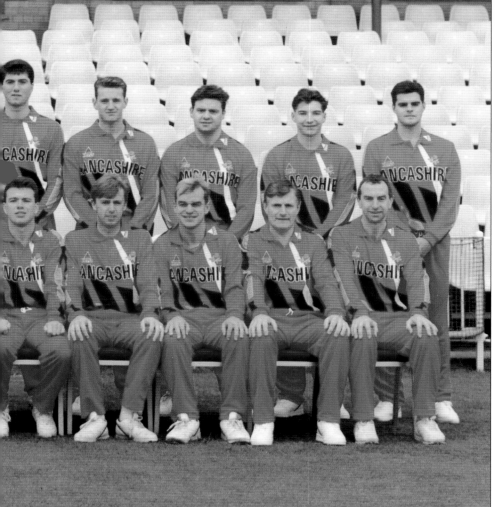

Above: The Second XI won the Bain Clarkson Trophy in 1990.

Back (l to r): John Savage (coach), John Crawley, Nick Derbyshire, Marcus Sharp, Steve Titchard, Ronnie Irani, Ian Austin, Mark Crawley, Gary Yates, Tim Orrell, Ian Folley.
Front: Peter Martin, John Stanworth, Nick Speak, Dexter Fitton, Graham Lloyd, Tim Wallwork.

Left: In 1993 coloured clothing was introduced for the Sunday League. It its 25th year, the competition required a new image as crowds were dwindling. Lancashire's first outfit in the competition was predominantly red.

Back (l to r): Glen Chapple, Stewart Fletcher, Jonathan Fielding, Gary Yates, Steve Titchard, Marcus Sharp, Peter Martin, Ronnie Irani, Nick Derbyshire, Dexter Fitton, Mark Harvey, Alex Barnett.

Front: Lawrie Brown (Physio), Gehan Mendis, John Stanworth, Ian Austin, Mike Watkinson, Phil DeFreitas, Neil Fairbrother (capt), Mike Atherton, Warren Hegg, Nick Speak, Graham Lloyd, David Hughes (manager), David Lloyd (coach).

Above: **Neil Fairbrother** and **Mike Atherton** broke the record 3rd wicket partnership scoring 364 at the Oval against Surrey in 1990. Neil went on to make 366, the second highest individual score for Lancashire after Archie MacLaren. The innings closed at 863, the highest ever innings total for Lancashire.

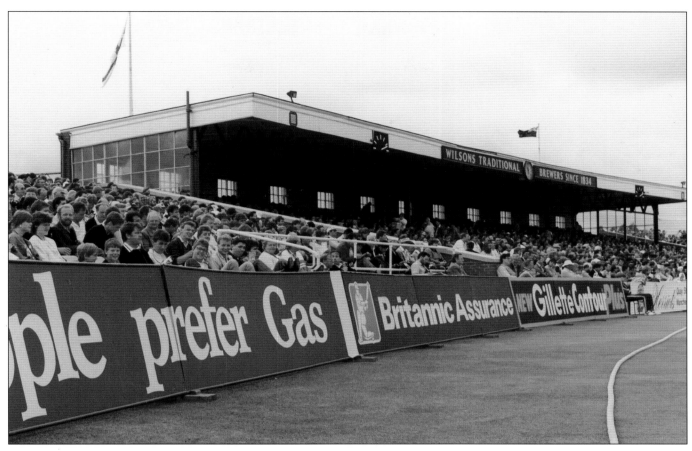

The old Wilson Stand (above) was demolished in 1992 and replaced by the double decker stand (below) in 1993.

Above: President Ken Cranston congratulates Cyril Washbrook and Winston Place on achieving 80 not out at Lancashire's AGM in December 1994.

The Lancashire Players Association was thriving. It enabled former players to meet socially and informally. Cricketers from the nineteen thirties to the eighties attended the functions regularly.

Right: The Hon Sec addresses Brian Statham, Roy Tattersall, Harry Pilling and Peter Lee.
Below right: Frank Hayes, Jack Dyson and Ken Shuttleworth catch up with the news.
Below: Duncan Worsley, Bob Berry, Jack Bond, Geoff Edrich and Arthur Booth.

Above: Modern cricket - **Mike Atherton** takes evasive action against the West Indian fast bowlers in 1995.

In 1995 Lancashire defeated Kent in the final at Lord's to win the Benson and Hedges Cup. It was Lancashire's fifth Lord's final in six seasons.

L to R. *Back:* Jason Gallian, Neil Fairbrother, Mike Atherton, Mike Watkinson (with Cup), Ian Austin, John Crawley, Gary Keedy, Nick Speak, Warren Hegg, Graham Lloyd, Steve Titchard. *Front:* Gary Yates, Glen Chapple.

Above: The team play football on the waterlogged field after an abandoned Sunday League game in September 1995.

Above: A jazz band entertains the crowd at the Test match.

Above left: The 'double' once again in 1996. Lancashire defeated Northamptonshire to retain the Benson and Hedges Cup at Lord's. **Mike Watkinson** lifts the trophy.

Above: **Wasim Akram**, one of Pakistan's greatest international bowlers with over 400 Test wickets, played for Lancashire from 1988-98. A left arm opening bowler, he took 374 wickets for the Club and played a key role in winning many one-day games.

Left: **Neil Fairbrother** captained Lancashire in 1992 and 1993. A consistently prolific left-handed bat, he is likely to record 20,000 first class runs for his County, only the second player (with Ken Grieves) to do so since the War. Neil has also scored well over 10,000 runs in one-day cricket.

Essex were skittled out for 57 leaving Lancashire with a victory by 129 runs in the 1996 NatWest Trophy final at Lord's.

Above: **Glen Chapple** takes 6 for 18 to record the best ever Lord's final bowling analysis.

Left: Captain **Mike Watkinson** (centre) with NatWest Man of the Match **Glen Chapple** (left) and B&H Man of the Match **Ian Austin.**

NatWest Trophy winners 1996 *L to R:* Glen Chapple, Peter Martin (Behind), Graham Lloyd, Gary Yates (hidden), Neil Fairbrother, Jason Gallian, Mike Watkinson (Capt), Ian Austin, Warren Hegg (hidden), Nick Speak, John Crawley, Richard Green (Front), Steve Titchard, Steve Elworthy.

The concrete trough used for housing the large protective cover was filled in at the end of the 1996 season and the heat inflated cover (pictured below) was cut up and used for sheeting to protect the wicket.

Above: In July 1996 **Jason Gallian** scored 312 against Derbyshire at Old Trafford, the highest individual score at the ground by any player.

Above: In the winter of 1996-97 the new cricket centre was built. It is one of the largest in the world with five extra long lanes.

Left: Reception.

Below: Five extra long practice nets.

Below left: Conference rooms included.

The Pavilion was extended to fulfil safety requirements of a larger exit and lift. It was officially opened in April 1997 by the Chairman Bob Bennett and President Brian Statham.

Below: Twelve first class practice nets were completed for home and visiting teams on the old practice ground at the Stretford End.

Left: Lancashire were invited to play in Calcutta in January 1997 to commemorate the 50th anniversary of India's independence. The team won the Wills Trophy (below) beating India 'A' at Eden Gardens witnessed by almost 50,000 spectators.

Above: Lancashire won the Second XI Championship in 1997.
Back (l to r): Steve Titchard, Liam Bones, Paul Ridgway, Paddy McKeown, Chris Hall, Graham Lloyd.
Front: Mark Chilton, Gary Yates, Peter Sleep (Captain and Coach), Chris Schofield, Jamie Haynes.

In 1998, Lancashire won the NatWest Trophy at Lord's beating Derbyshire by nine wickets.

Back (l to r): Glen Chapple, Graham Lloyd, Warren Hegg, John Crawley, Wasim Akram (Captain), Neil Fairbrother, Mike Atherton, Peter Martin, Ian Austin, Gary Yates.

Front: Andrew Flintoff, Mark Chilton, Dav Whatmore (Coach).

Above: Twenty-four hours after success in the NatWest Trophy the team won the AXA sponsored one day league trophy.
Back (l to r): Andrew Flintoff, Peter Martin, Mark Chilton (hidden), Neil Fairbrother, Glen Chapple, Wasim Akram (Capt), John Crawley (hidden), Graham Lloyd, Ian Austin, Gary Yates. *Front:* Warren Hegg, Dav Whatmore.

1998 was an excellent year for Lancashire who also finished runners-up in the Championship.

A new media centre was built on the executive boxes.

Above: From this...
Left: ... to this.

Above: A sell out for the World Cup semi-final in June 1999 played at Old Trafford when Pakistan beat New Zealand. The newly built Old Trafford lodge is seen on the right of the Pavilion.

Left: Viewing from the 68 bedroom Old Trafford Lodge opened in April 1999.

In 1999 the National Cricket League one day competition was sponsored by CGU and was split into two divisions. Lancashire finished the season as National League Champions.

Right: The team celebrate as Warren Hegg and Neil Fairbrother spray the champagne.

Below right: Captain **John Crawley** with the well earned trophy.

Below: The Lancashire v Yorkshire CGU League floodlit match attracted a crowd of well over 12,000.

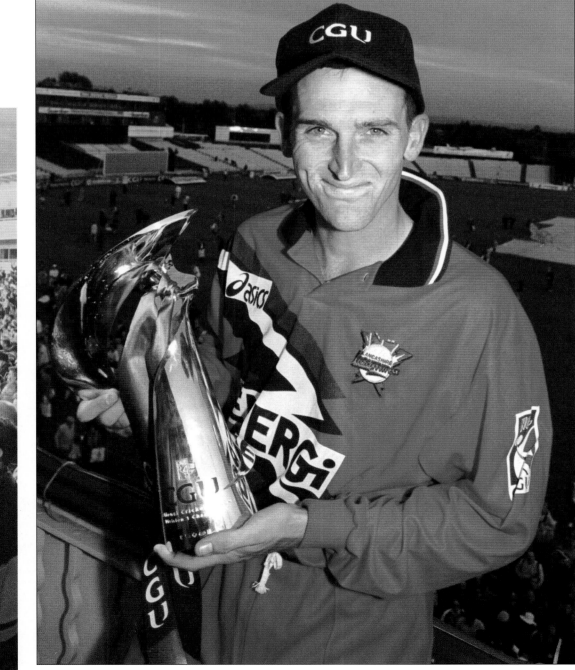

Above: In 1999, his first season at Old Trafford, the Sri Lankan overseas professional **Muttiah Muralitharan** bowled in only six first class matches yet captured 66 wickets at a mere 11.7 runs per wicket, helping Lancashire to finish runners-up in the Championship.

Right: Overseas professional for the 2000 season **Sourav Ganguly** of India scored almost 800 runs in one day cricket for Lancashire.

England contracts were awarded for the first time in the 2000 season and three Lancashire players were signed up; batsman **Mike Atherton**, all-rounder **Andrew Flintoff** and leg spinner **Chris Schofield**.

Left: Mike Atherton.

Below: Chris Schofield.

Right: Andrew Flintoff.

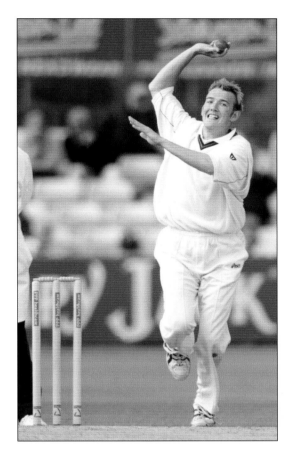

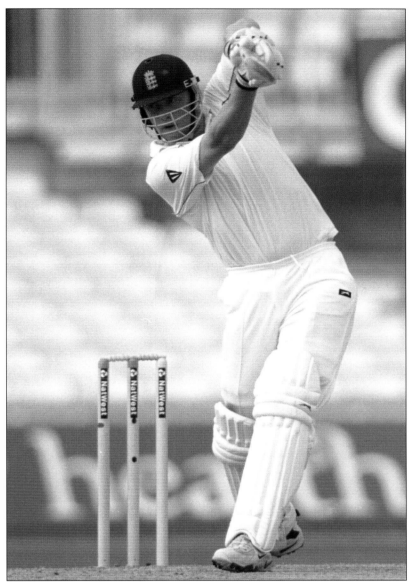

Right: Lancashire's **Mike Atherton** and Surrey's Alec Stewart receiving their 100th Test Cap at Old Trafford on August 3rd, 2000, England v West Indies.

In September 2000 Lancashire's wicket-keeper **Warren Hegg** passed George Duckworth's 634 catches in first class cricket to set up a new record for his County.

Left: Warren Hegg.

Below: A proud Hegg receives the warmest congratulations from his team mates after breaking Duckworth's record.

In the NatWest Trophy at the Oval in July 2000, **Andrew Flintoff** made Lancashire's highest individual score in the history of the competition with an unbeaten 135 from 110 balls. Andy also holds the Lancashire record in the National (Sunday) League, hitting 143 off only 66 balls against Essex in 1999.

Old Trafford has undergone many changes since 1857. Ground development will continue and growing business activities will support the cricket and maintain the team as a premier side in Britain. Without doubt Lancashire CCC has a bright future.

List of Subscribers

Ref	Subscriber	Favourite Player	Ref	Subscriber	Favourite Player
001	Keith Hayhurst, Cheadle Hulme	Brian Statham	070	H. Gordon Storey, Twyford	Clive Lloyd
002	Les Morgan, Bury	Cyril Washbrook	071	Bryan J. Gisbourne, Pleasington	Clive Lloyd
003	Michael A. Coop, Worsley	Cyril Washbrook	072	Graham Maskell, Mossley	Clive Lloyd
004	Brian Shaw, Poulton-Le-Fylde	Brian Statham	073	M.J. Crosbie, Orton Longueville	Brian Statham
005	R.A. Godfrey, Wrexham	Brian Statham	074	William Taylor, Formby	Jack Simmons
006	Norman Burrows, Ainsdale	Brian Statham	075	Prof. Ray Hill, Eccles	Brian Statham
007	Leonard Whatmough, London	Eddie Paynter	076	Stephen Lonsdale Finch C.B.E., Fareham	Cyril Washbrook
008	Brian A. Robinson, Brentwood	Brian Statham	077	Joseph H. Urmson, Glossop	Brian Statham
009	Dr Ian McKinley, Irlams O' Th' Height	Brian Statham	078	Andrew J. Ashton, Oldham	Graeme Fowler
010	Nigel Schooler, Birmingham	Geoff Pullar	079	Derek Carter, Burnley	Neil Fairbrother
011	Christopher Miller, Ilford	Clive Lloyd	080	Jamie R. Carter Burnley	Neil Fairbrother
012	Howard S. Berry, Bury	Harry Pilling	081	Steven Farrell, Stretford	Jack Simmons
013	Philip Hall, Bolton	Cyril Washbrook	082	Raymund N.P. Carroll, Didsbury	Brian Statham
014	Ken Jefferson, Rawtenstall	Brian Statham	083	A.W. Laughton, Rainow	Brian Statham
015	Arthur Pendlebury, Ribbleton	Brian Statham	084	Graeme Gardner, Clayton-Le-Woods	Neil Fairbrother
016	Roland Stuart, Broughton in Furness	Brian Statham	085	Alan J.J. Smith, Old Windsor	Jack Ikin
017	Robert Allan Harrison, Nelson	Brian Statham	086	Brian H. Rhodes, Winwick	Clive Lloyd
018	Thomas W. Barton, Chorley	Clive Lloyd	087	Lee Markey, Monton	Mike Watkinson
019	R.C. Wright, Leyland	Brian Statham	088	Mr A.E.H. Mason, Adlington	Brian Statham
020	David Hill, Cramlington	Neil Fairbrother	089	William Fearick, Tyldesley	Cyril Washbrook
021	John B. Diggle, Macclesfield	Brian Statham	090	John Littler, Belgrave Park	Brian Statham
022	Stephen John Lewin, Warrington	Paul Allott	091	H. Howard, Bramhall	Brian Statham
023	Anthony Clive Davies, Dobcross	Michael Atherton	092	Andy Russell, Saffron Walden	Ken Higgs
024	William A. Powell, Hemel Hempstead	W. Brearley	093	R.K. Boothman, Teddington	Neil Fairbrother
025	Brian R. Phillips, Liverpool	Brian Statham	094	Nicholas J. Miller, Widnes	Mike Watkinson
026	Graham John Bromage, Offerton	Farokh Engineer	095	Colin Pimlott, Southport	Neil Fairbrother
027	Jack Shone, Killington	Brian Statham	096	Colin Blakeley, Bolton	Brian Statham
028	Rodney Pitchford, Liverpool	Brian Statham	097	Melvyn M. Owen, Churchtown	Michael Atherton
029	Charles Cooke, Nantwich	Brian Statham	098	Stan Price, Manchester	Brian Statham
030	Mark Timothy Blaker, Whitton	Brian Statham	099	John George Tyror O.B.E., J.P., Knutsford	Cyril Washbrook
031	Keith Davies, Prestbury	Tom Greenhough	100	Mrs Lesley McHutchon, Didsbury	Frank Hayes
032	Steven Richmond, Liverpool	J. Clarke	101	David Beeley, Badminton	Farokh Engineer
033	John Lloyd Morris, Urmston	Harry Pilling	102	Mrs Pat Glover, Middleton	Cyril Washbrook
034	Albert Smith, Denton	Brian Statham	103	Philip Brown, West Derby	Ezra Nutter
035	George Baines, Sheffield	Brian Statham	104	Lee McCabe, Wheelton	Mike Watkinson
036	Edward Aldersley, Hawkshaw	Brian Statham	105	Alan W. Lowndes, Penrhyn Bay	Clive Lloyd
037	Peter M. Farrow, London	Clive Lloyd	106	R.T. Ross, Liverpool	
038	Robert Edward Holmes, Heaton Mersey	Clive Lloyd	107	Matthew Gareth Vaughan, Swinton	Michael Atherton
039	Malcolm & Loraine Philp, Mitcham	Mike Watkinson	108	Alan Jubb, Ashton-under-Lyne	Jack Bond
040	William B.C. Lister, Southport	Eddie Paynter	109	Brian Smith, Oldham	Brian Statham
041	Jim Nuttall, Great Harwood	Brian Statham	110	Leonard Mollineux, Manchester	Clive Lloyd
042	Alan G. Harrison, Roe Green	Clive Lloyd	111	Stanley Sharples, Bolsover	Brian Statham
043	Anthony J. Appleby, Blackpool	Brian Statham	112	George Frederick Bennett Hall, Isle Of Man	
044	John Carey, Burnham	Jack Simmons	113	John Brough, Westhoughton	Brian Statham
045	Mitch Booth, Wombourne	Clive Lloyd	114	Brian White, Bury, Lancashire	
046	John B. Corless, Warrington	Cyril Washbrook	115	Don Ambrose, Ribchester	Brian Statham
047	Graham Haworth, Church	Brian Statham	116	Christopher T. Howe, High Crompton	Cyril Washbrook
048	Barry Horton, Prestwich	Clive Lloyd	117	J. Michael May, Woking	Cyril Washbrook
049	W.H. Oddie, Burnley	Johnny Briggs	118	Henry T. Tattersall, Bishopsteignton	Brian Statham
050	Glyn Williams, Stalybridge	Clive Lloyd	119	Stanley James Corr, Poulton-Le-Fylde	Clive Lloyd
051	Peter Hall, Heswall	Brian Statham	120	The Rt. Hon. Sir Robert Atkins	
052	Tony Bradley, Shaw	Clive Lloyd		M.E.P., Garstang	Archie MacLaren
053	George Taylor, Pendlebury	J. Ikin	121	Ted Longton, Lancaster	Geoff Pullar
054	Brian M.F. Ratcliffe, Droylsden	Brian Statham	122	D.J. Middleton, Nelson	Brian Statham
055	Norman Jump, Standish	Brian Statham	123	Leonard Arthur Collins, Worthing	Brian Statham
056	Frank Hitchen, Horwich	Brian Statham	124	Stuart Christie, Cressington Park	Cyril Washbrook
057	Jeffrey Wilkinson, Bolton	Jack Bond	125	Anthony M. Polak, Welwyn	Clive Lloyd
058	David Neale Reynolds, Marlow	Brian Statham	126	Dr Brian J. Edmondson, Wallingford	Brian Statham
059	Gwynfor Jones, Romiley	Brian Statham	127	David F. Rowson, Stockport	Clive Lloyd
060	Ron Burrows, Lostock Hall	Brian Statham	128	Anthony Roy Shaw, Appleton	Neil Fairbrother
061	Dr Ian Graeme Barrison, Harpenden	Brian Statham	129	Alan Hartill, Heaton Norris	Neil Fairbrother
062	Mr A.D. Halliwell, Douglas	Neil Fairbrother	130	David Peel, Hale	Brian Statham
063	Andrew Mooney, London	A.C. MacLaren	131	Gary Coleman, Unsworth	Michael Atherton
064	Trevor F. Vearncombe, Southport	Jack Simmons	132	Norman Collier, Tyldesley	Brian Statham
065	Stanley Hartley, Lytham	Brian Statham	133	S.T.F. Moore, Prestbury	David Lloyd
066	Leonard Cecil Irving, Lytham St Anne's	Cyril Washbrook	134	Michael J. Jones, Warwick	Clive Lloyd
067	Harry Duckworth, Hutton	Jack Simmons	135	Clive M. Jones, Golborne	Brian Statham
068	Trevor D. Thomas, Wallasey	Brian Statham	136	David John Arrowsmith, Burnley	
069	Allan Appleton, Kendal	Cyril Washbrook	137	Philip Thomas Pressler, Darwen	Clive Lloyd

Edmund Rowley
1864-1879

A.N. Hornby
1880-93, 1897-98

Sydney Crosfield
Joint Capt. 1892-1893

Archie MacLaren
1894-96, 1899-1907

Gerry Bardswell
Joint Capt. 1899

A.H. Hornby
1908-1914

Myles Kenyon
1919-1922

Jack Sharp
1923-1925

Leonard Green
1926-1928

Ref	Subscriber	Favourite Player
138	Chris Golding Claines	Jack Simmons
139	Roy B. Sumner, Egerton	Brian Statham
140	Keith Francis, Caton	Clive Lloyd
141	Anthony Benson, Lancaster	Jack Simmons
142	Howard David Oldroyd, Quernmore	Cyril Washbrook
143	Professor Ian Isherwood C.B.E., Disley	Cyril Washbrook
144	I.D.G. Mills, Sale	Cyril Washbrook
145	Peter J. Wilkinson, Leyland	Brian Statham
146	Phil Garlington, Preston	
147	Mike Hill, Chorlton	Graeme Fowler
148	Sean Grovestock, Walkden	Brian Statham
149	Alan Brown, Worsley	Brian Statham
150	Stephen Bostock, Ramsbottom	Brian Statham
151	John Michael Dixon, Wrington	Clive Lloyd
152	David John Baker, Lostock	Brian Statham
153	Philomena C. Hageman, Netherlands	Michael Atherton
154	Dr. William John Jackson Legg Lytham St. Anne's	Brian Statham
155	Nigel John Halsall, Blackpool	Michael Atherton
156	Nicholas Jude Lindsay, Macclesfield	
157	Air Vice Marshal G.C. Lamb CB,CBE,AFC,FBIM, R.AF.(retd) Berkhamsted	Cyril Washbrook
158	Peter John Jones, Penwortham	Neil Fairbrother
159	Michael D. Moore (The Roses Hat), Morecambe	Neil Fairbrother
160	Paul Kerfoot, Preston,	Warren Hegg
161	Richard John Martin, Chester	Michael Atherton
162	Michael W. Roberts, Stockport	Brian Statham
163	Gareth P.W. Roberts, Stockport	Gary Yates
164	Andrew M.W.Roberts, Stockport	Jack Simmons
165	Geoff Walker, Liverpool	Cyril Washbrook
166	Kevin Richard Kitchen, Fleetwood	Wasim Akram
167	Mr Eddie Newcomb, Chelsea	Brian Statham
168	Edith Ritchie, Berkhamsted	Jack Simmons
169	Roland T. Adams, Stretford	Brian Statham
170	John D. Carr	
171	Steve Hughes, Liverpool	Wasim Akram
172	David Hodgkiss, Bolton	Brian Statham
173	Mr Robert Geoffrey Lewis Andrews, Holmes Chapel	Michael Atherton
174	Gary Chadwick, Tottington	Clive Lloyd
175	David W. Ashall, Thelwall	Clive Lloyd
176	Norman Barton, Blackburn	Brian Statham
177	Neil Barton, Great Harwood	Harry Pilling
178	Dr. Ian Graeme Barrison, Harpenden	Brian Statham
179	George Baines, Sheffield	Brian Statham
180	Mr J.H. Urmson, Glossop	Brian Statham
181	Stuart Christie, Liverpool	Cyril Washbrook
182	Stanley Sharples, Bolsover	Brian Statham
183	Brian Finlow, Macclesfield	Cyril Washbrook
184	R. A. Godfrey, Wrexham	
185	Christopher J. Parsons, St Helens	Michael Atherton
186	Arthur Morgan, Tarvin, Chester	Michael Atherton
187	Kenneth Hardacre, Rochdale	Brian Statham
188	Eric Midwinter, Harpenden	Harry Pilling
189	Keith F. Kirkman, Potton, Beds.	Clive Lloyd
190	Peter Halliwell, Knutsford	
191	David Frost, Wimbledon	
192	J. Stewart Kent, Clitheroe	So Many
193	Derek J.V. Whitehouse, Higher Blackley	Cyril Washbrook
194	Andrew L. Thorneley, Penrith	Brian Statham
195	James A. Thorneley, Penrith	Brian Statham
196	Bernice Sherwin, Moston	Brian Statham
197	John Creedon, Richmond	Clive Lloyd
198	Mr Eric Seal, Ormskirk	Clive Lloyd
199	Shona H. Towers, Chester	J.T. Ikin
200	Owen Widdup, Nelson	Cyril Washbrook
201	Mr John Brian Rawcliffe, Preston	Brian Statham
202	Bob Teague, Truro	Winston Place
203	Christopher Taylor, Northwich	Brian Statham
204	David Harris, London	Brian Statham
205	Matthew Daniels, Stockport	Wasim Akram
206	Timothy Finnie, Banbury	J. Briggs
207	Ronnie Hazlehurst, Guernsey	Brian Statham
208	J.K.F. Rigby, Worsley	Cyril Washbrook
209	Ken Medlock O.B.E., West Kirby	Jack Iddon
210	Richard A. Jones, Spital	Clive Lloyd
211	John Watson, Bollington	Mike Watkinson
212	Eric Rawson, Manchester	
213	Sir Norman Statham, Reigate	Brian Statham
214	Kenneth Moore, Shrewsbury	Michael Atherton
215	Stephen Davies, Accrington	Clive Lloyd

Ref	Subscriber	Favourite Player
216	John Wilkinson, Fulwood, Preston	Brian Statham
217	John Morris, Basingstoke	Jack Simmons
218	Brian J. Coombs, Sale	Brian Statham
219	Alan F. Sherris, Ramsbottom	Michael Atherton
220	Geoffrey Moorhouse, Hawes	Eddie Paynter
221	David Johnson, Wigan	Brian Statham
222	Mr Terence Kenny, St Helens	Neil Fairbrother
223	David Mason, Life Member, Salford	Brian Statham
224	Donald Foulds, Rochdale	Brian Statham
225	Mrs Edith Bennison, Accrington	Cyril Washbrook
226	Horace Foster, Grappenhall	Eddie Paynter
227	Gerard Meath, Stone	Brian Statham
228	J.K. Sedman, London	Cyril Washbrook
229	R. Keith Baines, Poulton-Le-Fylde	Brian Statham
230	Brian Guest, Pwllheli	George Duckworth
231	Dave Marsh, Rochdale	Brian Statham
232	Mr. W. G. Coulshed, Salisbury	Brian Statham
233	Dr Harry Hands, Southport	George Duckworth
234	Mr D.A. Roper, Culcheth	Cyril Washbrook
235	A. D. Mills, Southport	
236	Anthony McKenna, Stockport	Brian Statham
237	Martin John McKenna, Stockport	Clive Lloyd
238	Bernard Joseph McLoughlin, Macclesfield	Brian Statham
239	Charles Putnam, Stretford	Clive Lloyd
240	Thomas D.W. Astorga C.B.E., Glasgow	Cyril Washbrook
241	Mr Fred Hardman, Manchester	Brian Statham
242	Brian Walsh, Bourne	Brian Statham
243	Betty Windle-Boddy, Bolton	Clive Lloyd
244	Mr D. H. Smith, Royton	
245	E.I.Clark, Cheadle Hulme	Cyril Washbrook
246	Bryan E. Brown, Salford	Jack Ikin
247	John Alan Enser, Abersoch	Jack Iddon
248	Thomas Clifford Berry, Prestwich	G.E.Tyldesley
249	H. John Osborne, Appledore	Brian Statham
250	Richard H. Osborne, Moss Nook	Brian Statham
251	Martin Sixsmith, London	Clive Lloyd
252	Gina Hearn, London	David Lloyd
253	Colin Wood, Poulton-Le-Fylde	Brian Statham
254	Hugh Malcolm Carey, Peasemore	Clive Lloyd
255	Timothy Robert Collister, Blackpool	Wasim Akram
256	Alexander Butler Rowley, Frinton On Sea	Cyril Washbrook
257	B. H. Shann, Sale	Cyril Washbrook
258	Kevin Connolly, Royton	Brian Statham
259	John Howard Gartside, Droylsden	Clive Lloyd
260	H. M. Alty, Liverpool	Cyril Washbrook
261	Peter Kneale, Wavertree	Neil Fairbrother
262	John Wright, Hoylake	J.T. Ikin
263	John Watters, Knutsford	
264	Geoffrey Sharp, Formby	Jack Sharp
265	Ian Withers, Altrincham	
266	Carl Withers, Altrincham	
267	Vincent Fanning, Bradford	Brian Statham
268	Charles M. Oliver, London	Ernest Tyldesley
269	Dr. Jack Dunham, Coombe	Winston Place
270	Christopher Taylor, Hyde	Clive Lloyd
271	Fred Whitmore, Golborne	Brian Statham
272	Brian Collins, St Helens Recs CC	Neil Fairbrother
273	Eric Fazackerley, Preston	Brian Statham
274	Jack Holt, Manchester	
275	John Alan Hawkins, St Bees	Jack Ikin
276	R.E.M Haworth, High Wycombe	Cyril Washbrook
277	John Fazackerley, Bournemouth	Brian Statham
278	Mrs Phyllis Norton, Romiley	Neil Fairbrother
279	Malcolm Barber, Wallasey	Neil Fairbrother
280	Eddie Owens, Shotton	Cyril Washbrook
281	Dr. John Haworth, Carlisle	Brian Statham
282	Mr S.C. Gregory, Stretford	Brian Statham
283	Phillip Edward Miles, L.C.C.C. Superstore	Mike Atherton
284	Patrick G. Rogan, Belfast	Cyril Washbrook
285	Brian Barlow, Manchester	Frank Hayes
286	Sean & Jane Riley C.T.I.D., Chadderton	Gary Yates
287	James Ratcliffe, Bolton	Brian Statham
288	Stanley Hallows, Warrington	Wasim Akram
289	Moyra Hampson, Wilmslow	Brian Statham
290	Hugh Forgan, Altrincham	Brian Statham
291	James Duke, Highbury, London	Clive Lloyd
292	G.M. Richardson, Woking	J.T. Ikin
293	Brian Atkinson, Wigan	Brian Statham
294	Brian Howard, Great Missenden	Cyril Washbrook
295	Norman Richardson, Bolton	Richard Gorton Barlow
296	David Wildman, Burnley	Clive Lloyd
297	W.H. Hoole (Biographer, A.N. Hornby), Winsford	

Ref	Subscriber	Favourite Player
298	E.P.Wall, Nantwich	
299	Gary Hirst, Redditch	Neil Fairbrother
300	Mr David Wood, Morecambe	Clive Lloyd
301	Mr Karl Robert Marshall (Bob), Southport	Clive Lloyd
302	Jim Howe, Dukinfield	Brian Statham
303	Gordon Moss, London	Brian Statham
304	Brian William Fitzgerald, Cheshire	Cyril Washbrook
305	Neville Denson, St Bees	J.T. Ikin
306	Philip Bellamy, Marple Bridge	Brian Statham
307	Bryan Holmes, Cumbria	J.B. Statham
308	Leslie A. Taylor, Mossley	Clive Lloyd
309	Peter Edward Banks, Sale	Clive Lloyd
310	Harry Watkinson, Stretford	Brian Statham
311	Adrian Hay, Greenhithe	Michael Atherton
312	John Lyon, Oldham	
313	Francis Charles Farrell, Widnes	Eddie Paynter
314	William Miles, Cheadle	Cyril Washbrook
315	Rev. Joseph Cain, Manchester	Ernest Tyldesley
316	Peter David Higson, Blackburn	Clive Lloyd
317	Ron Davison, Rochdale	Brian Statham
318	Dr. P.I. Vardy, Runcorn	David Lloyd
319	David A. Bird, Sale	Brian Statham
320	Edward Bradshaw, Leigh	Brian Statham
321	Joe Holloway, Swinton	Ernie Tyldesley
322	Brendan Barker, Maidenhead	Clive Lloyd
323	Neil & Christopher Taylor, Bolton	Graeme Fowler
324	Dr. Jim Leeming, Manchester	Clive Lloyd
325	Peter Moss, St Helens	Clive Lloyd
326	Lawrence Wilkinson, Sale	Eddie Paynter
327	J Dalton, Manchester	Brian Statham
328	Walter Thorp, Leeds	Cyril Washbrook
329	J.B. Johnson, Edinburgh	J.B. Statham
330	Harvey Marsden, Wakefield	Eddie Paynter
331	Doug Savage, Manchester	Brian Statham
332	Charles M. Bridge, Stockport	Clive Lloyd
333	John Cunningham, Manchester	Cyril Washbrook
334	Reg Cass, Oldham	Clive Lloyd
335	W. Long, Billericay	
336	Tim Price, Lymm	Michael Atherton
337	Peter A. Sargent, Stretford	Graeme Fowler
338	James Brian Entwistle, Southport	Malcolm Hilton
339	Michael R. Tew, Poynton	Clive Lloyd
340	A. Ealden, Worthing	Michael Atherton
341	David H. Johnson, Preston	Jack Simmons
342	A.M. Lees, Stockport	Eddie Paynter
343	E.C. Lowe, Wigan	George Duckworth
344	Basil Murphy, North Woodchester	Cyril Washbrook
345	Peter Roberts, Silverdale	Clive Lloyd
346	Anthony Atkinson Place, Poulton-le-Fylde	Cyril Washbrook
347	Stanley A. Knowles, Chester	Brian Statham
348	Sylvia Bebbington, Stockport	Clive Lloyd
349	William Henry Finch, Preston	Brian Statham
350	David L. Barlow, Bolton	Cyril Washbrook
351	E.H. Kirk, Cilcain	A.C. MacLaren
352	Peter Cairns, Preston	Clive Lloyd
353	Mr J. Salisbury, Burnley	Harry Pilling
354	Malcolm Andrew, Poulton-le-Fylde	Brian Statham
355	Carol Chapple, Sedgley	David Lloyd
356	John Charnock, Warrington	Brian Statham
357	Jim Clarke, Blackburn	
358	Philip Thomas Jackson, Bolton	Jack Ikin
359	Chris Rowe, Wigan	Neil Fairbrother
360	W.E. Baldwin, Cherry Tree	Neil Fairbrother
361	Philip Ravensdale, Congleton	Brian Statham
362	Peter Moore, Hove	Winston Place
363	Mr D.E. Pilkington, Rochdale	J.B. Statham
364	Mary Evans (née Pilling), Ightham	Brian Statham
365	Steve Goodall, Cheadle	Graeme Fowler
366	Douglas Whalley, Cheadle	Clive Lloyd
367	F.C. Bakewell, Sale Moor	J.B. Statham
368	William Frank Fish, Rossendale	
369	Thomas Cooke, Fleetwood	Cyril Washbrook
370	Ann Moulton, Chorley	Michael Atherton
371	Neil Taylor, Burnley	Brian Statham
372	Richard S. Downs, Hale	Brian Statham
373	John Clifford, Wirral	Cyril Washbrook
374	Peter Bebbington, Wrenbury	Brian Statham
375	Jack S. Borrows, Wirral	Brian Statham
376	J.W. Sutton, Oswestry	Brian Statham
377	J.D.B. Cook, Clackmannan	J.B. Statham
378	Philip Leonard Richardson & Anne James, Stoke on Trent	J.T.Ikin

Ref	Subscriber	Favourite Player
379	Mr Cecil Wood, Manchester	Cyril Washbrook
380	Michael Kennedy, Manchester	Clive Lloyd
381	Robert Joseph Charlton, Crewe	Cyril Washbrook
382	Gil Howarth, London	Clive Lloyd
383	David Lathrope, Matlock	Brian Statham
384	Mr R.A. Alves, Altrincham	Clive Lloyd
385	Mr Jim Dinnage B.A. (HONS), Bolton	Michael Atherton
386	Roy Ashurst, Wigan	George Duckworth
387	Harvey Williams, Mold	Clive Lloyd
388	John Alan Davies, London	Jack Simmons
389	Martin Wharton, Newcastle upon Tyne	
390	Anthony N. Mackay, Sale	Brian Statham
391	Albert Phythian, St Helens	Farokh Engineer
392	Geoffrey H. Hughes, Cheadle	
393	P.G. Taylor, London	Ernest Tyldesley
394	Mr R.G. Hardie, Bramhall	Brian Statham
395	Richard Dean, Hartford	Robert Barber
396	Dorothy M. Vernon, Dent	Brian Statham
397	A.R. Webster, Maghull	Cyril Washbrook
398	Bernard Law, Manchester	Brian Statham
399	Harry Funge, Bramhall	
400	George Anderton, Haydock	Brian Statham
401	James Fraser, Blackburn	Bill Roberts
402	Peter McGuire, Read	Brian Statham
403	Peter Furlong, Warrington	J. Ikin
404	R.S. Pickup, Iver Heath	Michael Atherton
405	Edward Brian Nicol, Lancaster	Brian Statham
406	Brian Groves, London	Cyril Washbrook
407	Murray Birnie, Rossendale	Clive Lloyd
408	James J. Billington, Lincoln	Brian Statham
409	Matthew Harrison, Bolton	Neil Fairbrother
410	Peter Stafford, Bolton	Winston Place
411	Colin Wood (deceased), Buxton	Clive Lloyd
412	Jonathan Pendlebury, Bolton	Brian Statham
413	Sally Wadsworth, Hove	Clive Lloyd
414	H. Cronkshaw, Preston	Eddie Paynter
415	Robert F.W. Cook, Halifax	Cyril Washbrook
416	Mark Finnigan, Sheffield	Bernard Reidy
417	Tony Briscoe, Southend-on-Sea	Clive Lloyd
418	Michael Briscoe, Bishops Stortford	Clive Lloyd
419	Lorraine Lewin, Warrington	Peter Martin
420	Garry Robinson, Leigh	Clive Lloyd
421	Stuart Brodkin, Edgware	Warren Hegg
422	Ian White, Frodsham	Clive Lloyd
423	A.A. Brookes, Godley, Hyde	Cyril Washbrook
424	P.J. Gause, Bury	Michael Atherton
425	Mike Billington, Manchester	Clive Lloyd
426	Dr. Dudley Hathaway, Birkenhead	Brian Statham
427	Charles MacMillan, Manchester	
428	David Sleight, Glasgow	Michael Atherton
429	Ian M. Roberts, Manchester	Clive Lloyd
430	Jonathan Maginess, Nantwich	Michael Atherton
431	Vic Ashley, Nantwich	Brian Statham
432	Kevin G. Bebb, Heaton Chapel	Michael Atherton
433	Paul Butterworth, Heaton Chapel	Michael Atherton
434	John Houghton, Brighouse	David Hughes
435	David Stephen Littler, Warrington	Michael Atherton
436	C. & D. Tomlinson, Bolton	Warren Hegg
437	M.R. Alton, Wilmslow	Muttiah Muralitharan
438	Eric Rowson, Leigh	
439	Carl G. Riggall, Manchester	Clive Lloyd
440	Robert Livingstone, Huddersfield	Brian Statham
441	Ann-Marie Chantler, Warrington	Clive Lloyd
442	Mark Jones, Waverton	
443	Neil McPhail, Manchester	Clive Lloyd
444	H.S. Davies, Hale Barns	Neil Fairbrother
445	A.S. Freeman, Firswood	Clive Lloyd
446	R. Watson, Seaham	Clive Lloyd
447	Barry Taylor, Bentham	John Sullivan
448	Derek Hodgson, Ilkley	David Green
449	Frank Johnson, Ashurst	Cyril Washbrook
450	Winnie & Wilf Black, Chorlton	Jack Bond
451	Colin Trenbirth, Bebington	Clive Lloyd
452	Brian Gardener, North End, Henley-on-Thames	Brian Statham
453	John Rhodes, Delph	Michael Atherton
454	Mr T.J. Robertson, Preston	Brian Statham
455	Barry Feeney, Hawkshead	Brian Statham
456	David Anthony Smith, Prestwich, Manchester	Clive Lloyd
457	Ruth Janice Witkin, Manchester	Clive Lloyd
458	R. Walker, Knott End-on-Sea	Michael Atherton
459	Brian Costin, Lytham	Clive Lloyd

Peter Eckersley
1929-1935

Lionel Lister
1936-1939

Jack Fallows
1946

Ken Cranston
1947-1948

Nigel Howard
1949-1953

Cyril Washbrook
1954-1959

Bob Barber
1960-1961

Joe Blackledge
1962

Ken Grieves
1963-1964

Brian Statham
1965-1967

Ref	Subscriber	Favourite Player
460	Dave Hooley, Accrington	Brian Statham
461	L. Sproston, Atherton	Peter Martin
462	Mr P.J.N. Padwick, Nantwich	
463	Mark Smith, Radcliffe	Rev. V.P.F.A. Royle
464	A.C.Kingston, Northampton	Jack Bond
465	Hugh Speller, Stockport	Michael Atherton
466	Y-Khow Wong, St Ives, Australia	Brian Statham
467	Eric Gwilt, Worsley	Brian Statham
468	Ron Smith, Bolton	Cyril Washbrook
469	Mrs S. Pollitt, Bolton-le-Sands	Brian Statham
470	Karl Brown, Atherton	Michael Atherton
471	Peter Ward, Thornton -Cleveleys	Michael Atherton
472	Roger Scholes, Lymm	Frank Hayes
473	Joe Morris, London	Neil Fairbrother
474	Terry & Jackie Morley, Stockport	Clive Lloyd
475	Keith Willans, Stockport	Brian Statham
476	T.V. Sykes, Dacre	R.H. Spooner
477	J.H. Delany, Dorchester	Cyril Washbrook
478	Peter W.G. Powell, Hemel Hempstead	Wasim Akram
479	Peter Gregory, London	Brian Statham
480	Glenn Fox, Rishton	Neil Fairbrother
481	Ian Scholes, Urmston	Neil Fairbrother
482	David Wright, Leyland	Neil Fairbrother
483	William H. Jones, Barrow-in-Furness	Brian Statham
484	R.D.J. Pilling, Bolton	Ian Austin
485	David Lloyd, Aintree	David Lloyd
486	David J. Wilson, Eccles	Neil Fairbrother
487	Barry Parker, St Helens	Clive Lloyd
488	Raymond Hill, Bolton	Clive Lloyd
489	Leonard Steinberg, Hale Barns	Cyril Washbrook
490	Phil Doyle, Liverpool	Michael Atherton
491	Michael Kirk, Walton	
492	David Brocklehurst, Manchester	Michael Atherton
493	James O'Reilly, Dublin	Eddie Paynter
494	Michael Frederick Tyrer, Winchester	
495	Dr. Don Hartley, Stanley	Brian Statham
496	Bruce D.N. Bricknell, Aberdeen	Clive Lloyd
497	John Leggatt, Oswestry	Alan Wharton
498	Mike Illsley, Perth	Clive Lloyd
499	T.P. Cranfield, Stockport	Brian Statham
500	Elizabeth Newell, Ilkley	Frank Hayes
501	Rev. Stuart Poole, Stockport	Jack Simmons
502	Roderick Hall, Manchester	Clive Lloyd
503	Bob Forrest, Manchester	Frank Hayes
504	Ian Verber, Yarm	Brian Statham
505	Donald Brown, Bebington	Brian Statham
506	Joan Jackson, Caton	Michael Atherton
507	Francis Baron, Rishton	Brian Statham
508	Stephen Jarman, Bolton	Cyril Washbrook
509	Mr Roy Higginson, Warrington	Jack Bond
510	C.J. Morton, Helsby	Brian Statham
511	Mike Lewis, Gatley	Roy Tattersall
512	W. Wardle, Rhyl	Brian Statham
513	Peter William Murphy, Thornton	Brian Statham
514	Derek Taylor, Stockport	Cyril Washbrook
515	Barrie Watkins, Worsley	Brian Statham
516	Terry C. Longworth, Bolton	Brian Statham
517	Graham Baron, Wigan	Brian Statham
518	David W. Matthews, St Helens	Clive Lloyd
519	Barry Rickson, Cheadle Hulme	Brian Statham
520	Mr Brian Peters, Leigh	Cyril Washbrook
521	Mr Keith Perry, Wimborne	Brian Statham
522	William Brooks, Leasowe	Brian Statham
523	David Croft, Sheffield	Clive Lloyd
524	F. Alan Kynaston, Mellor	Brian Statham
525	Thomas Barry Rice, Altrincham	Dick Pollard
526	Ronald J. Curtis, Higher Poynton	Clive Lloyd
527	Mike Saunders, Liverpool	Ian Austin
528	Raymond Cross, Whalley	Michael Atherton
529	C.P. Cooke, Crosby	Cyril Washbrook
530	Gordon Leff, Strensall	Brian Statham
531	John Brian Bowker, Middlewich	Harry Pilling
532	Paul Eric Pearce, Allerton	Neil Fairbrother
533	Jack Ledger, Sale	Clive Lloyd
534	Mr A. Marsland, Uppermill	J.T. Ikin
535	Philip & Julia Crookall, Nantwich	
536	Frank Shellien, Aintree	Clive Lloyd
537	Steven John Brook, Oldham	Ian Austin
538	Adam Clarke, Cheadle Hulme	Mike Watkinson
539	Timothy Martland, Worthing	Jack Simmons
540	Peter Smith, Widnes	Michael Atherton
541	P.B. Wrigglesworth, Blackpool	Brian Statham

Ref	Subscriber	Favourite Player
542	Steven Kennedy, Blackpool	Harry Pilling
543	Anthony Walker, Davenham	Farokh Engineer
544	Chris Gore, Streatham, London	Neil Fairbrother
545	Ken Thomas, Stockport	Brian Statham
546	Derrick Fletcher, Blackrod	Brian Statham
547	Des Platt, Rainhill	Wasim Akram
548	David Chaloner, Oldham	Clive Lloyd
549	Ian Broadbent, London	Ian Austin
550	Jimmy Jones, Salford	Mike Atherton
551	Rory Davis, Nantwich	
552	Erica & Ian Davis, USA	
553	W.K. Rigby, Preston	Cyril Washbrook
554	John H.A. Tate, Ainsdale	Johnny Briggs
555	Harold Gibson, Cwmbran	Harry Pilling
556	K.A. Sankey, Ormskirk	
557	Garry Clarke, Warrington	Warren Hegg
558	D.B. Cooper, Preston	Brian Statham
559	Stephen White, Lancaster	Neil Fairbrother
560	Frank Greenwood, Leigh	Brian Statham
561	Family of Ken Grieves, Whitefield	
562	Robert N. Taylor, Preston	Eddie Paynter
563	Daniel J. Clough, Darwen	Michael Atherton
564	Brian Reilly, Darwen	Cyril Washbrook
565	Mick Thexton, Preston	
566	Nick Berentzen, Old Harlow	Clive Lloyd
567	Harry Howarth, St Chads Cres, Uppermill	Brian Statham
568	Roger Mason, Mellis	
569	J.E.P. Kelly, Timperley	Clive Lloyd
570	Donald Whitehead, Oldham	Clive Lloyd
571	Mr K.A. Boardman, Rochdale	
572	Dave Dutton, Ireby	Brian Statham
573	Andrew N. Buckley, Craven Arms	David Hughes
574	Jack Fargher, Ashby-de-la-Zouch	Clive Lloyd
575	Mrs Anne Birch, Chepstow	Michael Atherton
576	Jack Beeson, Flixton	Brian Statham
577	Graham K. Beeson, Flixton	Neil Fairbrother
578	Prof. D. Ibbetson, Cambridge University	Michael Atherton
579	Roger Jolly, Winsford	
580	Bob Thomson, Gosport	Clive Lloyd
581	Norman Gee, Oldham	Cyril Washbrook
582	Ken Fielding, Bolton	Brian Statham
583	John. L.Q. Robbins, Leigh	J. T. Tyldesley
584	Derek Waters, Nantwich	Brian Statham
585	Bob Brady, Formby	David Lloyd
586	Dave Fletcher, Liverpool	Brian Statham
587	Howard W. Hulme, Macclesfield	Cyril Washbrook
588	Philip L. Hale, Walkden	Brian Statham
589	J. B. Gribbin, Barnsley	Brian Statham
590	George William Norris, New Barnet	Cyril Washbrook
591	J. E. Richards, Whitegate	Brian Statham
592	Alex Twells, Chorleywood	Cyril Washbrook
593	Robert O'Hara, Rossendale	J.T.Ikin
594	David Frodsham, Cirencester	Graeme Fowler
595	Derek Thomas, Malaysia	David Lloyd
596	Mark Hannon, Audenshaw	Neil Fairbrother
597	Russell Heath, Bolton	
598	Carey Randall, Red Rose Travel Club	Mike Watkinson
599	B. J. Rothwell, Chandlers Ford, Hampshire	Brian Statham
600	Daniel J. Parker, Wylam	Cyril Washbrook
601	Ian Farrington, Leyland	Ian Austin
602	Noel McKee, Carnforth	Cyril Washbrook
603	Lucy M. A. Voss, London	Brian Statham
604	Barrie Wood, Rossendale	Neil Fairbrother
605	David Tuck, Bolton	Ian Austin
606	James Peter Lee, Blackpool	Brian Statham
607	Michael Anthony Lee, Blackpool	Brian Statham
608	Andrew R. Leach, Skipton	Clive Lloyd
609	Eddy Cowen, Southport	Eddie Paynter
610	Geoffrey Thomas Chapman, Denton	Brian Statham
611	Alan Beeley, King's Lynn	Eddie Paynter
612	George Ince, Perthshire	Cyril Washbrook
613	Ron Helm, Timperley	Graeme Fowler
614	Mr David Peel, Manchester	
615	J. E. Arnold, Ashton	Clive Lloyd
616	Ronald A. Spriggs, Eyemouth	Jack Simmons
617	Oliver J. W. Kenyon, Glossop	Michael Atherton
618	Alan Hooley, Marple	Brian Statham
619	Karen Peers, Leyland	Neil Fairbrother
620	Ranjit Rajam, Brooklands	Clive Lloyd
621	Alan G. Hollinshead, Macclesfield	Brian Statham
622	Richard A. Hollinshead, Bollington	Jack Simmons

Ref	Subscriber	Favourite Player
623	John Pickles, Whitefield	Brian Statham
624	Neil Fallows, Little Lever	Brian Statham
625	John Pickerill, Newcastle Under Lyme	Clive Lloyd
626	Rev. Barry W. Newth, Bolton	Cyril Washbrook
627	Christopher David Smyth, Knutsford	Neil Fairbrother
628	Laurie Lancashire, Bury	Brian Statham
629	J.O. Jones, Deganwy	Brian Statham
630	Donald Conway Davis, Gerrards Cross	Brian Statham
631	David Woods, Wigan	
632	John Nicholson, Bolton	Brian Statham
633	Dr. John A. Horsfield, Levenshulme	Brian Statham
634	R. Blackhurst, Kirby	Clive Lloyd
635	H. N. Greenwood, Cambridge	
636	Mary D. Pietsch, Northwich	Brian Statham
637	Andrew Roberts, Great Sutton	Neil Fairbrother
638	David Allan Robertson, Morecambe	Brian Statham
639	Mr Gerald Hudd, Warrington	Brian Statham
640	Bill Evans, Llandynan	Brian Statham
641	John Gambles, Rhewl	Brian Statham
642	Peter N. Formstone, Bromborough	Brian Statham
643	B. W. Gibbard, Warrington	Cyril Washbrook
644	John C. Crosby, Altrincham	Brian Statham
645	Ken Wild, Nantwich	Cyril Washbrook
646	Roy S. Smith, Hertford	Brian Statham
647	David Baldwin, Chorley	Harry Pilling
648	Peter Lawton, Old Trafford	Clive Lloyd
649	Mr John Burrow, Penwortham	Clive Lloyd
650	Robert Gordon Beveridge, Darwen	Brian Statham
651	Kenneth Barker, Stockport	Brian Statham
652	Mike McHugh, Croydon	Brian Statham
653	Christopher Critchlow, Guildford	Brian Statham
654	Elliot James Spencer, Macclesfield	Andrew Flintoff
655	John David Haydon, Great Sutton	Ian Austin
656	Miss Alwyn Gardner, Bolton	Brian Statham
657	James Nockels, North Harrow	Brian Statham
658	Jack Cresswell, Rochdale	Cyril Washbrook
659	David Muldoon, St Helens	David Lloyd
660	J. C. Bennett, Nantwich	Brian Statham
661	Kevan Royle, Goostrey	Cyril Washbrook
662	George W. Norris, Formby	Cyril Washbrook
663	Brian Butterworth, Rochdale	Brian Statham
664	Malcolm McLaren, Perthshire	Brian Statham
665	Francis G. Smith, Preston	Brian Statham
666	Michael Shenton, Macclesfield	Michael Atherton
667	Steven Forster, Altrincham	Harry Pilling
668	Arthur Maltby, Wirral	Dick Pollard
669	Geoff Hewitt, Preston	G.E. Tyldesley
670	Geoffrey Pinder, Stalybridge	Clive Lloyd
671	Alan Pinder, Bury	Clive Lloyd
672	D. E. Eaves, Preston	Brian Statham
673	P. W. Tomlinson, Macclesfield	Clive Lloyd
674	Christopher S. Shenton, Bushey Heath	Neil Fairbrother
675	Philip H. Barratt, Stockport	Brian Statham
676	Mr Vincent. C. McCann, Bury	Clive Lloyd
677	Jim Entwistle, Prestbury	Clive Lloyd
678	Alan Sollory, Warrington	Clive Lloyd
679	Martin Doyle, Cheadle Hulme	Clive Lloyd
680	Arthur Rushton, Swinton	Clive Lloyd
681	George Alexander Dickinson, Flackwell Heath	Brian Statham
682	Brian Ford, Hyde, Cheshire	
683	Gerald Woods, Matfield Green	Cyril Washbrook
684	John D. Wallace, West Kirby	Brian Statham
685	David A. H. Longstaffe, Nantwich	Cyril Washbrook
686	Edward Briggs, Swinton	Brian Statham
687	Colin Richard Jones, Plymouth	Clive Lloyd
688	Mr A. B. Nightingale, Preston	Jack Ikin
689	Paul B. French, Banbury	Clive Lloyd
690	Mike Smith, Bolton-by-Bowland	Michael Atherton
691	Arthur Fred Mayers, Worsley	Cyril Washbrook
692	Stephen Hignett, Winsford	Michael Atherton
693	Ian W. Greenwood, Preston	Clive Lloyd
694	Stephen Messenger, Wilmslow	Wasim Akram
695	Colin Chambers, Kelsall	Clive Lloyd
696	Mike Daly, Lancaster	Clive Lloyd
697	Kevin O,Neill, Stockport	Neil Fairbrother
698	Derek H. Wiles, Rochdale	Eddie Paynter
699	Paul Hinson, Sale	Clive Lloyd
700	Mr & Mrs Harrison, Windermere	Cyril Washbrook
701	Norman Riley, London	Cyril Washbrook
702	Alan Bretherton, Leyland	Brian Statham
703	Cyril J. O'Reilly, Preston	Harry Pilling

Ref	Subscriber	Favourite Player
704	David Spencer, Wilmslow	Brian Statham
705	Donald Watkinson & Ernest Noel Forshaw, Roby Mill	Brian Statham
706	Mr Gerald Cooper, Oldham	Brian Statham
707	Brian Williams, Grappenhall	Roy Tattersall
708	John P. Simpson, Walkden	Clive Lloyd
709	Ellis Clarke, Preston	Brian Statham
710	Graham Clarke, Whitby	Clive Lloyd
711	Kathleen Halstead Black, Liverpool	Brian Statham
712	James Rodney Cadman, Swinton	Cyril Washbrook
713	L. W. Jenkinson, Bolton	J. T. Ikin
714	Barrie Woodcock, Southport	Michael Atherton
715	John Maguire, Fleetwood	Cyril Washbrook
716	M. K. Brookfield, West Kirby	Cyril Washbrook
717	Steve Parker, Upton	Clive Lloyd
718	Noel P. King, Northolt	Clive Lloyd
719	N. G. Kaye, Anglesey	Ken Cranston
720	Jack Lomax, Arnside	Clive Lloyd
721	Eric G. McIntyre, Stockport	Brian Statham
722	E. Dabbs, Blackpool	Brian Statham
723	A. Kelly, Stretford	Brian Statham
724	Anthony Leech, Stisted	Michael Atherton
725	Michael Clarke, Wigan	Clive Lloyd
726	Alan L. Stott, West Kirby	Brian Statham
727	Ian Birchall, Wigan	Clive Lloyd
728	Andrew Neil Wilson, Poulton-le-Fylde	Clive Lloyd
729	Ron Dickson, Stockport	Brian Statham
730	Mrs Moreen Braley, Ormskirk	Brian Statham
731	Roger Ian Gaskell, Stockport	Brian Statham
732	Mr Keith Balmforth, Oldham	Brian Statham
733	David Cox, Chadderton	Cyril Washbrook
734	Michael John Rothwell, Chorley	Clive Lloyd
735	Doris Parkinson, Bromborough	Cyril Washbrook
736	Mike Worthington, Newcastle	Brian Statham
737	Frank Hampson, Wigan	Brian Statham
738	Gideon F. Drake, Mobberley	Cyril Washbrook
739	Margaret M. MacInnes, Llandudno	
740	Thomas Whiteside, St Annes	Clive Lloyd
741	Joseph A. Musgrave, Tarporley	Eddie Paynter
742	Alec D. Robertson, Jersey	Brian Statham
743	R. I. Rimmer, Poole	Cyril Washbrook
744	W. H. Forrester, Worcester	Eddie Paynter
745	Jane Catherine Penswick, Leyland	Neil Fairbrother
746	Mr David W. Taylor, Wrexham	Brian Statham
747	David Swain, St Helens	Brian Statham
748	Simon Taylor, London	Neil Fairbrother
749	Stanley Thomas Taylor, Liverpool	Clive Lloyd
750	David Hart, Liverpool	Brian Statham
751	Tim Barker, York	Michael Atherton
752	Mrs Betty Nolan, Ashtead	
753	Mr. B. A. Harrison, Pinner	
754	Gordon James Darlington, Macclesfield	Neil Fairbrother
755	W. I. Corlett, Marple	
756	Harold. G. Longstaff, Rainhill	Eddie Paynter
757	Alexander William Shaw, Sale	Cyril Washbrook
758	Mrs Brenda Ilett, Hyde	Brian Statham
759	Robin Meijer Mulvihill, Chester	Neil Fairbrother
760	Alistair John Law, Oxton	Jack Bond
761	Paul Turner, Lowton	Brian Statham
762	David G. Hilton, Atherton	Clive Lloyd
763	J.R.H. Battersby, Lytham St. Anne's	Cyril Washbrook
764	Michael J. Tully, Scorton	Brian Statham
765	Roy B. Sumner, Egerton	Brian Statham
766	Chris Goulding, Worcester	Jack Simmons
767	Linda A. Lees (née Bennett), Wigan	David Hughes
768	R.A. Lund, Scunthorpe	Cyril Washbrook
769	Richard McCombe, Kew	Brian Statham
770	Keith Ellison, East Grinstead	Sidney Barnes
771	Edith Butterworth, Milnrow	
772	W.D. Griffiths, Wrexham	Brian Statham
773	Dyfed Williams, Wrexham	Brian Statham
774	Clive R. Garston, Hale	J.B Statham
775	Daniel Murphy, Firswood	Farokh Engineer
776	Aidan Coughlan, Norwich	Michael Atherton
777	Paul Speller, Bredbury	Clive Lloyd
778	Mark Speller, Bredbury	Clive Lloyd
779	Ian Speller, Bredbury	Clive Lloyd
780	Graham Elkes, Denton	Clive Lloyd
781	Geoff Peel, Manchester	Michael Atherton
782	C.L. & K. Patrick, Urmston	John Abrahams
783	Wilf Longthorne, Rochdale	Brian Statham
784	John T. Brewer, Deddington	Cyril Washbrook

Jack Bond
1968-1972

David Lloyd
1973-1977

Frank Hayes
1978-1980

Clive Lloyd
1981-83, 1986

John Abrahams
1984-1985

David Hughes
1987-1991

Neil Fairbrother
1992-1993

Mike Watkinson
1994-1997

Wasim Akram
1998

John Crawley
1999-date

Ref	Subscriber	Favourite Player
785	John Haworth, Urmston	Clive Lloyd
786	David C. Thornton, Orwell	Clive Lloyd
787	Dr. D.W. Oldfield, Wilmslow	Cyril Washbrook
788	W. Lowe, Clifton	Farokh Engineer
789	R. Bradshaw, Clitheroe	Brian Statham
790	Larry Owen, Liverpool	Clive Lloyd
791	Peter Sheppard, Woodplumpton	Cyril Washbrook
792	Gillian G. Etherington, Sale	Jack Simmons
793	John Clarke, Aigburth	Brian Statham
794	R. Jones, Whalley Range	Frank Hayes
795	Dorothy M. Grant, Bowdon	Brian Statham
796	Simon Roger Holding, Bolton-le-Sands	Neil Fairbrother
797	Edward McMinn, Sale	Brian Statham
798	Harry Winsor, Merseyside	Brian Statham
799	Michael John Whelan, Disley	Brian Statham
800	J. F. Henry, Chorley	Cyril Washbrook
801	John Gray, Stretford	Graeme Fowler
802	Philip Orme, Liverpool	Clive Lloyd
803	John Jordan, Bewdley	Brian Statham
804	Cyril Fletcher, Heywood	Brian Statham
805	Harold Gee, Kelbrook	Brian Statham
806	Michael Richardson, Scotforth	Cyril Washbrook
807	Phil Bradbury, Urmston	Neil Fairbrother
808	Stephen W. J. Lyddon, Ormskirk	John Crawley
809	Arthur Batchelor, Brisbane, Australia	Michael Atherton
810	Paul D. Colquhoun, Sale	Brian Statham
811	Geoffrey A. Shindler, Manchester	Brian Statham
812	Mike Buxton, London	Brian Statham
813	Mrs Dorothy M. Hilton, Cape Town, South Africa	Cyril Washbrook
814	Michael William Horner, Heald Green	Clive Lloyd
815	Stuart A. Evans, Crumpsall	Brian Statham
816	John David Hadfield, Kettleshulme	
817	Jack Fitzgibbon, Stretford	Brian Statham
818	Dennis O. Smith, Skipton	Jack Bond
819	Stuart Spencer Sugh	Wasim Akram
820	Keith Fantom, Romiley	Michael Atherton
821	Eric Coplowe, Birkdale	Brian Statham
822	Bert Rigby, Stockton Heath	Cyril Washbrook
823	Tom Hargreaves, Blackburn	Michael Atherton
824	Graham F. Smith, Didsbury	Farokh Engineer
825	Joe Lever, Preston	Cyril Washbrook
826	Rev. Colin Arthur Powell, Manchester	Chris Schofield
827	David Monks, Prestwich	Brian Statham
828	Mrs Eileen Austin, Offerton	David Lloyd
829	John Blackburn, Bamber Bridge	Clive Lloyd
830	George Thomas, Horsham	Brian Statham
831	Michael John Smith, Deganwy	Michael Atherton
832	Roy Mullings, Macclesfield	Jack Simmons
833	Anita Wright, Worksop	Neil Fairbrother
834	Charles P. Wood, Barrow-in-Furness	Brian Statham
835	Philip Lea, Holywell	Mike Watkinson
836	Trevor Peacock, Bolton	Clive Lloyd
837	Tony Peacock, Bolton	Brian Statham
838	Rodney Stephens, Farnborough	Brian Statham
839	Bob McKenzie, West Calder	Frank Hayes
840	Geoff Hindle, Lancashire	Clive Lloyd
841	Craig Hindle, Lancashire	Neil Fairbrother
842	G.E. McGowen, Littleport	Brian Statham
843	Mike Dobbin, London	Clive Lloyd
844	Beatrice E. Thomas, Wigan	Geoff Pullar
845	John Morton, Urmston	Brian Statham
846	Keith Morton, Sale	Cyril Washbrook
847	Geoffrey E. Waite, Colinton	Clive Lloyd
848	Alan Chadwick, Altrincham	Brian Statham
849	Michael Ashton, Bromborough	Brian Statham
850	A. T. Thomas, Littleborough	Brian Statham
851	Ron Hudson, Hyde	J. B. Statham
852	Peter Thorne, Burnley	Graeme Fowler
853	Joan M. Smith, Manchester	Brian Statham
854	Philip Sherwin, Stoke-on-Trent	Clive Lloyd
855	Joseph Andrew Hornsby, Rossendale	Andrew Flintoff
856	Simon Nicholas Chapman, Astley	Clive Lloyd
857	Colin Smith, Bramhall	Cyril Washbrook
858	Graham Oldfield, Radcliffe	Mike Atherton
859	John Tomlin, Billinge	Barry Wood
860	Trevor Neale Watson, Kirkham	Brian Statham
861	Malcolm Gray, Ainsworth	Dick Pollard
862	A. Colclough, Oldham	Neil Fairbrother
863	Geoff Perkins, Warrington	John Abrahams
864	Steven Butterworth, Bredbury	Andrew Flintoff
865	Samuel A. Gifford, Old Trafford	Clive Lloyd

Ref	Subscriber	Favourite Player
866	Miss Eth Orton, Droylsden	Cyril Washbrook
867	Nick Magnall, Newton Heath	Ian Austin
868	Paul Eckersley, Derby	David Lloyd
869	Richard Fairbrother, Lancashire	Neil Fairbrother
870	Alan Jones, Cardiff	Neil Fairbrother
871	Peter David Gordon Ross, Macclesfield	Brian Statham
872	David S. Thompson, Burnage	Jack Simmons
873	Philip J.B. Gallagher, Bolton	Clive Lloyd
874	William Heaton Mortimer, Burnley	Jack Jordan
875	Mrs S. Kermode, Standlake	Cyril Washbrook
876	Mr G. Anthony Whittaker, Stoke Poges	Brian Statham
877	John F.H. Haskins, Cheadle	Clive Lloyd
878	Mr Graham C. Cunningham, Surrey	Neil Fairbrother
879	Stephen Ringrow, Marple Bridge	Neil Fairbrother
880	Paul Mackle, Salford	David Hughes
881	Stephen Robert Heyes, Westhoughton	Clive Lloyd
882	John R. Hoyle, France	Neil Fairbrother
883	Stuart Roberts, 1st XI scorer Littleborough CC	Clive Lloyd
884	Alan Donald Sharples, Southport	Sourav Ganguly
885	Robert Ibbison, Poulton-le-Fylde	Brian Statham
886	Paul Harrison, Penwortham	Clive Lloyd
887	J.B. Chantler, Winsford	Cyril Washbrook
888	Hugh Sheppard Bayley, Ashtead	Cyril Washbrook
889	Keith Gooch, Cranleigh	Brian Statham
890	Jeff Corry, Gatley	Neil Fairbrother
891	Mr Stephen D. Faulkner, Droylsden	Wasim Akram
892	Dave Pennington, Bramhall	Clive Lloyd
893	Chris Illsley, Tickhill	Brian Statham
894	John N. Allott, Hale	
895	Malcolm C. Dutchman-Smith, Penrith	Noddy Pullar
896	Michael H. Helm, Formby	Cyril Washbrook
897	Alan Johnson, Stockport	Clive Lloyd
898	Eric Gannon, Grappenhall	Clive Lloyd
899	Derek Charles Atherton, Rainhill	Brian Statham
900	Jack C. Bailey, Hazel Grove	Clive Lloyd
901	Alan Usher, Maghull	Warren Hegg
902	Daniel George Eadie, Bowdon	Neil Fairbrother
903	Geoff Homer, Timperley	John Sullivan
904	David W. Homer, Stretford	Cyril Washbrook
905	Patrick Miskell, Lancashire	Brian Statham
906	Frank Holmes, Great Harwood	Clive Lloyd
907	Mr D.A. Lambert, Prenton	
908	G.W. Seabury, Tattenhall	Eddie Paynter
909	Harry Lamb, Abergele	Cyril Washbrook
910	Andrew Lamb, Croydon	Cyril Washbrook
911	Joshua Holgate, Disley	Gideon Holgate
912	Ian Cruickshank, Urmston	Jack Simmons
913	John Pickavance, Haughton Green	Eddie Paynter
914	Michael Corkill, London	Cyril Washbrook
915	Paul Corkill, Liverpool	Cyril Washbrook
916	Evelyn Rhodes, Newburgh	Brian Statham
917	E.W. Jones, Newburgh	Brian Statham
918	Mark Stansfield, Burnage	Michael Atherton
919	Brian Higgs, Prenton	Graeme Fowler
920	Andrew Wang, Ware	Ken Higgs
921	Stuart Fife, Hawkshead	Jack Bond
922	James Outram, Calver	Michael Atherton
923	E.N. Freeman, Denton	Neil Fairbrother
924	D.W. O'Brien, Smithills	Michael Atherton
925	Kenneth N. Leatherbarrow, Swinton	Cyril Washbrook
926	Steven Williams, Little Eaton	Muttiah Muralitharan
927	Alan M. Senior, Sevenoaks	Brian Statham
928	Dennis Carradus, Bowerham	Cyril Washbrook
929	Frank M. James, Wrexham	Farokh Engineer
930	Sam Charles, Sale	Clive Lloyd
931	David John Taylor, London	
932	John Bailey Smith, ex Marple CC	Brian Statham
933	Trevor Charles Kingston Owen, Wimbledon	Clive Lloyd
934	Ronald Lord, Shaw	
935	Alan J. Marsh, Hazel Grove	Farokh Engineer
936	P.R. Clausen-Thue, Walton-on-Thames	Brian Statham
937	Ray Riley, Leigh	Jack Simmons
938	Glynne Davies, LCCC Development Association	Jack Bond
939	Adam J. Syddall, Bolton	
940	Matthew P. Syddall, Bolton	
941	Dennis Peyton, Ponders End	Clive Lloyd
942	Peter Laight, Hemel Hempstead	Bob Barber
943	Peter O'Connor, Cheadle Hulme	Clive Lloyd
944	Stephen Griggs, Wooten Wawen	Barry Wood
945	Kenneth Griggs, Lowton	Clive Lloyd

Ref	Subscriber	Favourite Player
946	Lucy & Betty Hall, Grange-over-Sands	
947	John Speak, Blackrod	Clive Lloyd
948	Granville Boden, Astley	Jack Ikin
949	Jack Howarth, Eccles	Eddie Paynter
950	Peter Robertson, Wallasey	Malcolm Hilton
951	A. Ken Taylor, Lowton	
952	Roland Edward Finney, Accrington	Brian Statham
953	Robert Meall, Newton-le-Willows	Cyril Washbrook
954	Phil Riding, Runcorn	F.M. Engineer
955	John D. Perry, Chorlton-cum-Hardy	Ian Austin
956	John Tarbuck, Blackburn	Clive Lloyd
957*	Philip L. Tarbuck, London	Neil Fairbrother
958	J. Michael Tarbuck, Warton	Clive Lloyd
959	John C. Kirkham, Shipley	Clive Lloyd
960	Malcolm Calvert, Handforth	Brian Statham
961	Paul Chauveau, Truro	Graeme Fowler
962	Peter Ashbrook, Stockport	Cyril Washbrook
963	Gwen Manchester	Wasim Akram
964	Stuart Casson, Brisco	Cyril Washbrook
965	John Shaw, Manchester	Brian Statham
966	Robert A. Lowrey, Stretford	Brian Statham
967	Susan Booth, Ormskirk	
968	Paul A. Green, High Lane	Brian Statham
969	Christopher William Elston, Greasby	Reginald Wood
970	Michael Craven, Mickle Trafford	Brian Statham
971	Mrs May Platt, Tyldesley	Jack Simmons
972	Ian Penney, Hazel Grove	Clive Lloyd
973	R.E. Richardson	
974	Stuart Foulds, Arnside	Harry Pilling
975	A.S. Alexander, Hale	Cyril Washbrook
976	John A. Heathcote, Leigh	Brian Statham
977	Dr. Gwyn Jones, Spondon	Brian Statham
978	Keith Topping, Lytham St. Anne's	Jack Bond
979	Christopher Bent, Warrington	Mike Atherton
980	David Butler, Blackpool	Graeme Fowler
981	Jack Fahey, Hoghton	Brian Statham
982	Edward G. Stanley, Littleborough	Clive Lloyd
983	Michael Lloyd, Hove	Jack Simmons
984	Paul Winrow, Bolton	Clive Lloyd
985	Tom Taylor, Worsley	Brian Statham
986	Gerald H. Milburn, Harwood	Brian Statham
987	Mr Len Scott, President E.C.C.,	Brian Statham
988	Brenda Evans, Handforth	John Ikin
989	Raymond Machell Q.C., Bowdon	Brian Statham
990	Alan Holmes, Denton,	Brian Statham
991	David James Maguire, Walton-le-Dale	Neil Fairbrother
992	Darroll N. Wike, Blackburn	Michael Atherton
993	John & Jean Roberts, Morecambe	Brian Statham
994	Maria Roberts, Broadbottom	Michael Atherton
995	David Allen McHoul, Prenton	Brian Statham
996	Colin Fishwick, Withington	Clive Lloyd
997	Dani Phillips, Manchester	Clive Lloyd
998	Godfrey Julian Phillips, Halsall	Brian Statham
999	J.R.E. Lyon, Manchester	Cyril Washbrook
1000	Ken Grime, Greenmount	Clive Lloyd
1001	R.A. Mawdsley, Lytham	Andrew Flintoff
1002	G.R. Mawdsley, Winchburgh	Frank Hayes
1003	Dr. Eve Mawdsley, Winchburgh	John Crawley
1004	Anthony McGowen, Urmston	Michael Atherton
1005	Michael Halford Clark, Macclesfield	S.F. Barnes
1006	John F. McPartlin, Edinburgh	Geoff Pullar
1007	Joseph Howley, Rawtenstall	Clive Lloyd
1008	Mr Mark Thomas, Old Colwyn	Bernard Reidy
1009	Peter Green, High Peak	Brian Statham
1010	Sarah Berman, Didsbury	Michael Atherton
1011	Bernard Jordan, Hazel Grove	Brian Statham
1012	Bryan Irvine, Falkirk	Geoff Pullar
1013	Stephen Clark Kirk, Firswood	Clive Lloyd
1014	Adrian Brodkin, Hampstead Garden Suburb	Clive Lloyd
1015	George Manley, Stretford	Clive Lloyd
1016	Simon Joos, Bury	Ian Austin
1017	Patricia Starkey, Formby	Michael Atherton
1018	George Dutton, Lancashire	Brian Statham
1019	Harvey Barrett, Lancashire	Jack Simmons
1020	Nicky Burchill, Manchester	
1021	John M. Hamman, Knutsford	
1022	David Hill, Warrington	Brian Statham
1023	Gary Anthony Brooks, Droylsden	Neil Fairbrother
1024	Eric D. Hughes, Lymm	Eddie Paynter
1025	David Cartwright, Ampthill	Cyril Washbrook
1026	A.G. Wright, Denton	J.B. Statham
1027	Paul Duckworth, Edenfield	Neil Fairbrother
1028	Sam & Jack McClements, Cheadle	John Crawley
1029	Anton Russell, London, Surrey	Wasim Akram
1030	Mr D. Levens, Firswood, Manchester	Neil Fairbrother
1031	Philip Laker, Lancashire	Brian Statham
1032	Colin Clarke, Silverdale	Cyril Washbrook
1033	Mrs Elsie Cotton, Warrington	
1034	Mrs Rosemary White, Deddington	Michael Atherton
1035	Johnny Roscoe, Nottingham	Clive Lloyd
1036	Maxine Purcell, Poulton-le-Fylde	Clive Lloyd
1037	William H. Davidson, Abergele	Brian Statham
1038	Jean Glass Munslow, Haughton Green	John Ikin
1039	Peter Lindsay, Stockport	Clive Lloyd
1040	Mr John Bancroft, Blackburn	
1041	Ray Jones, Denton	Neil Fairbrother
1042	Martin Bibby, Ennerdale	Brian Statham
1043	Stewart R.W. Hale, Maghull	Michael Atherton
1044	Walter Hayes, San Francisco, USA	Warren Hegg
1045	George E. Hill, Macclesfield	Brian Statham
1046	Kevin Roberts, Auckland, New Zealand	Brian Statham
1047	J.W. Minkley, Lincoln	Brian Statham
1048	Peter Simpson, Accrington	John Ikin
1049	Brian Simpson, Shaw	Brian Statham
1050	Gordon Simpson, Accrington	Wasim Akram
1051	Jim Lloyd, Reddish	Jack Iddon
1052	Graeme Crew, Walton-le-Dale	Michael Atherton